Freedom of Speech and Employment Law

The law relating to freedom of speech has grown faster than any other area of employment law over the past decade. Press controversies over online speech, disputed claims to the Equality Act, and allegations of no-platforming have all had the effect of making this the most dynamic area of workplace law. This book provides an introduction to this changing area of law in Great Britain. The first part of the book explains the overarching principle of employment and free speech law; the second half provides detailed case studies in relation to the specific examples that most commonly come before the courts. The book will be an essential reference for students, academics, and professionals working in the areas of Employment Law, Human Rights Law, and Contract Law. The British example will be of interest to an international readership.

David Renton is a barrister at Garden Court Chambers and Professor of Legal Practice at SOAS, University of London, UK.

Freedom of Speech and Employment Law

Practice in the British Courts

David Renton

LONDON AND NEW YORK

First published 2025
by Routledge
4 Park Square, Milton Park, Abingdon, Oxon OX14 4RN

and by Routledge
605 Third Avenue, New York, NY 10158

Routledge is an imprint of the Taylor & Francis Group, an informa business

British Library Cataloguing-in-Publication Data
A catalogue record for this book is available from the British Library

Library of Congress Cataloging-in-Publication Data
Names: Renton, David, author.
Title: Freedom of speech and employment law : practice in the British courts / David Renton.
Description: Abingdon, Oxon [UK] ; New York, NY : Routledge, 2024. | Includes bibliographical references and index.
Identifiers: LCCN 2024032391 (print) | LCCN 2024032392 (ebook) | ISBN 9781032724249 (hardback) | ISBN 9781032724294 (paperback) | ISBN 9781032724263 (ebook)
Subjects: LCSH: Freedom of speech—Great Britain. | Freedom of expression—Great Britain. | Employers' liability—Great Britain. | Employees—Dismissal of—Law and legislation—Great Britain. | Labor laws and legislation—Great Britain. | Human rights—Great Britain.
Classification: LCC KD4110 .R46 2024 (print) | LCC KD4110 (ebook) | DDC 341.4101—dc23/eng/20240714
LC record available at https://lccn.loc.gov/2024032391
LC ebook record available at https://lccn.loc.gov/2024032392

ISBN: 978-1-032-72424-9 (hbk)
ISBN: 978-1-032-72429-4 (pbk)
ISBN: 978-1-032-72426-3 (ebk)

DOI: 10.4324/9781032724263

Typeset in Times New Roman
by Apex CoVantage, LLC

Contents

Preface

The subject of this book is the law in relation to freedom of speech and, in particular, the operation of that law by the courts in relation to workplace disputes. Although a wide range of primary and secondary legislation and caselaw is explained, at the core of this book is the recurring question of what different groups of people in the workplace should do in a situation where an employee has made, or is likely to make, speech which has or will be controversial, with other members of the workplace saying that the expression is unwanted and has distressed them. Should the employer punish, or should they dismiss? Should the employee apologise? Should they make a promise not to make comments of that same essential character again?

This book is an account of the existing law, not an attempt to develop it in a new direction.[1] Rather, the emphasis has been on studying the law as a totality, stating it as accurately as I can, and showing where the balance is currently found between the freedom of speakers to state their opinions and the right of their audience to receive information without having to suffer because something about that speech is likely to violate their own dignity.

I have written this book on the assumption that it will be consulted by dismissed employees and their representatives, by trade unionists, HR professionals, employers, and those who represent them. Each of those groups, I hope, will find something useful in the analysis that follows, in which I have set out the current state of the law and how judges have determined cases of these sorts in favour of different groups at different times.

There will be some people who read this book and use it to construct arguments of their own, portraying free speech as an essential and defining political virtue; I wish them every good fortune. In the same spirit, I also welcome anyone else reading this account if using it to argue that speech must moderate itself to take account of its audience. While there is some commentary in this

1 Any readers interested in my own positions on free speech are invited to consult a previous, more polemical work in which I addressed that question. D. Renton, *No Free Speech for Fascists: Exploring "No Platform" in History, Law and Politics* (London: Routledge, 2021).

book, I have deliberately restricted it, focussing rather on stating as accurately as I can just what the present law is.[2] It is an entirely healthy instinct to want to change the law. Before you can do that, though, you need to know what the law says.

2 This book was completed on 30 May 2024. I have attempted to state the law accurately as of that date. My thanks to the other members of the Employment Team at Garden Court who influenced the writing of this book, and, in particular, Oscar Davies, for their valuable comments on a first draft.

1 Freedom of expression

General principles

The right to freedom of expression is enshrined in UK law[1] in the European Convention on Human Rights ("ECHR", "the Convention"). The most important Convention right is article 10, which protects the right to freedom of expression.

The Convention is given effect by the Human Rights Act 1998 (see "Giving effect to Convention rights – in domestic law" further on.)

ARTICLE 10 AND FREEDOM OF EXPRESSION

Article 10 ECHR provides that:

(1) Everyone has the right to freedom of expression. This right shall include freedom to hold opinions and to receive and impart information and ideas without interference by public authority and regardless of frontiers. This Article shall not prevent States from requiring the licensing of broadcasting, television, or cinema enterprises.
(2) The exercise of these freedoms, since it carries with it duties and responsibilities, may be subject to such formalities, conditions, restrictions, or penalties as are prescribed by law and are necessary in a democratic society, in the interests of national security, territorial disorder or crime, for the protection of health or morals, for the protection of the reputation or rights of others, for preventing the disclosure of information received in confidence, or for maintaining the authority and impartiality of the judiciary.

1 The law which is summarised in this book is the law as it applies to England and Wales. Scotland has an Employment Tribunal system separate but akin to that of England and Wales. The main piece of legislation discussed in this book, the Equality Act 2010, applies in Scotland as it does in England. The Equality Act does not apply to Northern Ireland, which has a patchwork of overlapping equality laws.

DOI: 10.4324/9781032724263-1

The term "expression" includes the written word, the spoken word, web pages,[2] photographs,[3] art,[4] and the playing of live music.[5] It has also been held to include actions, such as a protest in a cathedral which consisted of a mixture of verbal and non-verbal expression,[6] and the hanging of dirty laundry on the railings of a national parliament.[7]

Article 10 protects not only the substance of the ideas expressed but also the form in which they are conveyed.[8] As the ECtHR explained in *Alekhina and Others v Russia*:

> The Court has also held that opinions, apart from being capable of being expressed through the media of artistic work, can also be expressed through conduct.[9]

The Courts have declined to limit the protection of free expression to words which were spoken with care or politely. Article 10 protected an anti-war activist who attended an airbase and defaced an American flag by writing on it the words, "Stop Star Wars".[10]

Receiving and imparting ideas

The right to freedom of expression ensures that individuals can access information to form their opinions. It protects them so that they can engage with others, for instance, to further develop their opinions, demand their rights, protest, or contribute to shaping the political landscape. Because article 10 protects the rights of people to receive information, a high degree of protection has been given to people whose work involves imparting information, including journalists, authors, politicians, lecturers, etc.

So, in the first case in which the ECtHR considered the weight to be given to article 10, Peter Lingens, a magazine editor, had in 1975 published two articles accusing the Austrian Chancellor Kreisky of being complicit with former Nazis. The state prosecuted Lingens for criminal libel. The ECtHR held that Lingens' article 10 rights had been infringed:

> Freedom of the press furthermore affords the public one of the best means of discovering and forming an opinion of the ideas and attitudes of

2 *R v Perrin* [2002] EWCA Crim 747, para 2.
3 *Douglas v Hello! Ltd* [2001] QB 967.
4 *Ashworth and Ors v The Royal National Theatre* [2014] EWHC 1176, para 27.
5 *Achbita v G4S Secure Solutions* [2017] EUECJ C-157/15, para 27.
6 *Alekhina and others v Russia* [2018] ECHR 616.
7 *Tatár and Fáber v Hungary* [2012] ECHR 1681.
8 *Jersild v Denmark* [1994] ECHR 33, para 31.
9 *Alekhina and Others v Russia* (2019) 68 EHRR 14, para 204.
10 *Percy v DPP* [2001] EWHC 1125, para 31.

> political leaders. More generally, freedom of political debate is at the very core of the concept of a democratic society which prevails throughout the Convention.[11]

In *Handyside v United Kingdom*, the author of 'Little Red Schoolbook' had published material discussing pornography, abortion, and drug use. The judges held that:

> Freedom of expression constitutes one of the essential foundations of a democratic society and one of the basic conditions for its progress and for the development of every man. It is applicable not only to information or ideas that are favourably received, but also to those that offend, shock or disturb the state or any sector of the population.[12]

The ECtHR has stated that "Democracy thrives on freedom of expression"[13] and that "freedom of political debate is at the very core of the concept of a democratic society which prevails throughout the Convention".[14] "There is little scope under Article 10 of the Convention for restrictions on political speech or on debate of matters of public interest".[15]

In *Alekseyev v Russia*,[16] the ECtHR held that Russia had violated the Convention by refusing to allow Gay Pride marches to take place in Moscow. Russia insisted that a ban was necessary because of the fear of disorder from far-right groups. The Court held that if every risk of conflict during a demonstration were to warrant its banning, society would be unable to hear views which offended majority opinion.

In *Matuz v Hungary*,[17] a journalist was dismissed for breach of confidentiality after publishing a book accusing his employee, the state broadcaster, of censorship. The ECtHR held that a fair assessment of an applicant's article 10 rights required considering: (a) whether there was any public interest in the information disclosed; (b) whether the information disclosed was authentic; (c) the damage suffered by the employer as a result of its disclosure; (d) the motive of the employee in disclosing the information; (e) whether the information had been made public as a last resort, following disclosure to some other superior or competent body; and (f) the severity of the sanction imposed on the employer.

In whistleblowing cases, the leading decision of the Human Rights Court is *Guja v Moldova*. That case provides that, in deciding whether article 10 protects an employee from dismissal for whistleblowing, the key considerations

11 *Lingens v Austria* (1986) 8 EHHR 407, para 42.
12 *Handyside v United Kingdom* [1976] EHRR 737, para 49.
13 *Centro Europa 7 SRL and Di Stefano v Italy* [2012] ECHR 974, para 129.
14 *Lingens v Austria*, para 42.
15 *Wingrove v United Kingdom* [1996] ECHR 60, para 58.
16 *Alekseyev v Russia* (2019) 69 EHRR 16, para 77.
17 *Matuz v Hungary* [2015] IRLR 74, para 34.

are likely to be: whether or not alternative channels for the disclosure were available; the public interest in the disclosed information; the authenticity of the disclosed information; the detriment to the employer; whether the whistleblower acted in good faith; and the severity of the sanction.[18]

A number of declarations of principle by the highest UK courts confirm that the right to freedom is an essential foundation of democracy. In *R v Central Television.* The Claimant had a conviction for child sex offences. He argued that a television report of the criminal investigation should not proceed. It would lead to the identification of his blameless wife and child. Lord Justice Hoffman said that if freedom of expression limited itself to what Judges thought responsible, it would be no freedom at all. Hoffman LJ said that:

> It cannot be too strongly emphasised that outside the established exceptions or any new ones which Parliament may enact in accordance with its obligations under the Convention, there is no question of balancing freedom of speech against other interests. It is a trump card which always wins.[19]

In *Young, James and Webster v United Kingdom*, it was said that the pluralism of individual interests is central to the functioning of a legitimate democracy:

> [P]luralism, tolerance and broadmindedness are hallmarks of a "democratic society". . . Although individual interests must on occasion be subordinated to those of a group, democracy does not simply mean that the views of a majority must always prevail: a balance must be achieved which ensures the fair and proper treatment of minorities and avoids any abuse of a dominant position.[20]

In *R v Shayler*, a former member of the Security Service was charged with breaches of the Official Secrets Act. At a preliminary hearing, Moses J had ruled that there was no public interest defence available under that Act. In the House of Lords, Lord Bingham restated the "fundamental" importance of article 10 to British democracy.

> Modern democratic government means government of the people by the people for the people. But there can be no government by the people if

18 *Guja v Moldova* [2008] ECHR 144, paras 79–96; for the operation of this test since, see *Heinisch v Germany* [2011] IRLR 922; *Halet v Luxembourg* [2023] ECHR 947. While this guidance was formulated to assist courts in resolving whistleblowing cases, UK courts have drawn on these principles in other cases where an employer has passed on information but is not, on the strict application of domestic law, a whistleblower. *Hill v Governing Body of Great Tey Primary School* [2013] EAT 0237/12, and see Chapter 2.

19 *R v Central Independent Television plc* [1994] Fam 192, 203.

20 *Young, James and Webster v United Kingdom* (1989) 11 EHRR 439, para 112.

> they are ignorant of the issues to be resolved, the arguments for and against different solutions and the facts underlying those arguments.[21]

In *Animal Defenders International,* Lord Bingham held that "The free communication of information, opinions and argument about the laws which a state should enact and the policies its government at all levels should pursue is an essential condition of truly democratic government". Article 10 plays a "central role in the Convention", protecting "free speech in general and free political speech in particular".[22]

In *Reynolds v Times Newspapers* (1999), the House of Lords held that the protection to free expression under the common law and the Convention were the same.[23]

Permitted interference with expression

Article 10(2) makes freedom of expression a qualified right. It emphasises not just the rights of a speaker but their responsibilities to other people. Under Article 10, "restrictions" may be made on expression "as are prescribed by law and are necessary in a democratic society".

The principle of freedom of expression ceases to apply if the language used is contrary to the law. This happens when an expression is so offensive it is criminal (for example, because the words used are threats of violence) or it is in breach of civil law (for example, because the expression is libellous or discriminatory, etc.).

In *Sporring and Lonroth v Sweden,*[24] the judges observed that their task in applying the two limbs of article 10 was a balancing exercise:

> The Court must determine whether a fair balance was struck between the demands of the general interest of the community and the requirements of the protection of the individual's fundamental rights. The search for this balance is inherent in the whole of the Convention.

In *Perinçek v Switzerland,* the Grand Chamber of the European Court of Human Rights considered the case of a Communist journalist in Turkey who

21 *R v Shayler* [2002] UKHL 11, para 21. Bingham accepted Moses J's reasoning, but not without first having set out the opportunities for a former member of the security services to seek to disclose supposed official secrets and their entitlement to challenge by judicial review any decision of the Minister refuse them permission and the obligation of the judges in those circumstances to apply the proportionality test, favourable as that was to article 10 freedom of expression.

22 *Animal Defenders International, R (on the application of) v Secretary of State for Culture, Media, and Sport* [2008] UKHL 15, para 27; also *R (ex parte Prolife Alliance) v BBC* [2004] 1 AC 185, para 6.

23 *Reynolds v Times Newspapers Ltd and others* [1999] UKHL 45; also *R v Secretary of State for the Home Department* (2000) 2 AC 115, 126.

24 *Sporrong and Lonroth v Sweden* (1982) 5 EHRR 35, para 73.

had denied that the killing Armenians in 1915 had amounted to genocide, insisting that the Western powers had been culpable and ordinary Turks innocent. The journalist was prosecuted and fined for his remarks. The Court held by ten votes to seven that his conviction infringed article 10, with several factors telling in the journalist's favour: his denial of genocide had not been accompanied by any demands for hatred or intolerance against Armenians; there had been no heightened tensions in Switzerland at the time he gave his remarks; no international-law obligations required Switzerland to criminalise them, the effect of the judgments of the Swiss courts had been to criminalise the defendant effectively for voicing an opinion that diverged from established opinion in Switzerland. Accordingly, it had not been necessary, in a democratic society, to make such speech criminal.[25]

Overlap with article 9, religion or belief

Also relevant to the protection of freedom of expression under the European Convention on Human Rights is Article 9 of the Human Rights Convention. That article protects the right of people to hold opinions, which it makes absolute: "Everyone has the right to freedom of thought, conscience and religion".

The second sentence of Article 9 makes the manifestation of religious belief a qualified right, doing so in terms similar to article 10(2):

> Freedom to manifest one's religion or beliefs shall be subject only to such limitations as are prescribed by law and are necessary in a democratic society in the interests of public safety, for the protection of public order, health or morals, or for the protection of the rights and freedoms of others.

In the case of *Sahin v Turkey*, the European Court of Human Rights provided clear guidance on the foundational nature of the rights in article 9 as well as the basis for the limitations which may be placed on those rights:

104. . . . as enshrined in Art.9, freedom of thought, conscience and religion is one of the foundations of a "democratic society" within the meaning of the Convention. This freedom is, in its religious dimension, one of the most vital elements that go to make up the identity of believers and their conception of life, but it is also a precious asset for atheists, agnostics, sceptics and the unconcerned. The pluralism indissociable from a democratic society, which has been dearly won over the centuries, depends on it . . .

106. In democratic societies, in which several religions co-exist within one and the same population, it may be necessary to place restrictions on freedom

25 *Perincek v Switzerland* (2016) 63 EHRR 6, para 280.

> to manifest one's religion or belief in order to reconcile the interests of the various groups and ensure that everyone's beliefs are respected . . .
>
> 108. Pluralism, tolerance and broadmindedness are hallmarks of a "democratic society". Although individual interests must on occasion be subordinated to those of a group, democracy does not simply mean that the views of a majority must always prevail: a balance must be achieved which ensures the fair and proper treatment of people from minorities and avoids any abuse of a dominant position.[26]

The ECtHR has held that the protection provided by articles 9 and 10 of the Convention is "closely linked".[27]

The freedom to hold whatever belief one likes goes hand-in-hand with the state remaining neutral, as between competing beliefs. The government must ensure that groups opposed to one another tolerate each other. It must refrain from expressing any judgment as to whether a particular belief is more acceptable than another.[28]

In the 1982 case of *Campbell and Cosans v United Kingdom*, the ECtHR considered an application from two parents whose children attended state schools in Scotland and objected to the schools' use of corporal punishment. At issue in the case was whether the parents' opposition to such punishment qualified as a protected belief. The Court held that the phrase "religious and philosophical convictions" could not apply to any opinions whatsoever but only "views that attain a certain level of cogency, seriousness, cohesion and importance" and "convictions as are worthy of respect in a democratic society".[29]

Since then, beliefs which have been found to come within article 9: the Hare Krishna movement,[30] Jehovah's Witnesses,[31] pacifism,[32] Communism,[33] atheism, and agnosticism.[34]

The courts are slow to interrogate the validity of another person's belief. As Lord Nicholls said in the 2005 cases of *Williamson*:

> [E]mphatically, it is not for the court to embark on an inquiry into the asserted belief and judge its 'validity' by some objective standard such

26 *Sahin v Turkey* (2007) 44 EHRR 5.

27 *Ibragimov v Russia*, application nos 1413/08 and 28621/11, para 78.

28 *Metropolitan Church of Bessarabia v Moldova* (2002) 35 EHRR 13, paras 115–16.

29 *Campbell and Cosans v United Kingdom* (1982) 4 EHRR 293, para 36. For whether belief counts as protected in UK law, in particular anti-discrimination law, see Chapter 2.

30 *Iskcon v United Kingdom* (1994) 76A DR 90.

31 *Kokkinakis v Greece* (1994) 17 EHRR 397.

32 *Arrowsmith v United Kingdom* (1978) 19 DR 5, para 71.

33 *Vogt v Germany* (1996) 21 EHRR 2015, para 60.

34 *Kokkinakis v Greece*, para 31. Such beliefs also come within section 10(2) Equality Act 2010: "Belief means any religious or philosophical belief and a reference to belief includes a reference to a lack of belief".

> as the source material upon which the claimant founds his belief or the orthodox teaching of the religion in question or the extent to which the claimant's belief conforms to or differs from the views of others professing the same religion. Freedom of religion protects the subjective belief of an individual . . . [R]eligious belief is intensely personal and can easily vary from one individual to another. Each individual is at liberty to hold his own religious beliefs, however irrational or inconsistent they may seem.[35]

Article 9 is a qualified right, subject to such limitations as prescribed by law and necessary. The distinction between a belief and its manifestation has become a recurring theme of the article 10 caselaw and is discussed at various points in what follows.

One of the recurring debates concerns whether, under article 9, manifestations require any protection at all. This has been debated most often in relation to religious clothing, but similar reasoning has been applied to an employee whose employer unfairly limits the expression of the manifestation of their religion in the workplace. So, in the veiling case of *Begum*, it was held that a pupil who was ordered to remove a headscarf could nevertheless "observe his or her religion without undue hardship or inconvenience".[36]

Other senior judges have, however, criticised this hard distinction between beliefs, which are protected under article 9, and manifestations, which are seemingly not. The counter-argument was put by Lord Justice Mummery in *Copsey v WWB Devon Clays,* a case in which an employee made working on Sunday obligatory to the discomfort of a Christian employee:

> The rulings are difficult to square with the supposed fundamental character of the rights. It hardly seems compatible with the fundamental character of Article 9 that a person can be told that his right has not been interfered with because he is free to move on, for example, to another employer, who will not interfere with his fundamental right, or even to a condition of unemployment in order to manifest the fundamental right.[37]

The extent to which manifestation of belief is itself protected is a recurring theme of this book, and I will return to the treatment of the issue in Chapters 6 and 7 to show how the majority of our senior judiciary presently see the question – their present perspective appears to be closer to Lord Justice Mummery than it is to Lord Nicholls.

35 *R v Secretary of State for Education and Employment ex parte Williamson* [2005] UKHL 15, para 22.
36 *Begum, R (on the application of) v Denbigh High School* [2006] UKHL 15, para 23.
37 *Copsey v WWB Devon Clays Ltd* [2005] EWCA Civ 932, para 35.

Giving effect to convention rights – in domestic law

The Convention is given effect in our domestic law by the Human Rights Act 1998.[38] Section 2(1) of HRA 1998 requires the courts to 'take into account' Convention case law if relevant. This means that ECtHR cases do not have to be followed *per se*, but they must be taken into account when domestic judges come to decisions in courts/tribunals. Domestic judges still have the discretion not to follow ECtHR decisions, though this is infrequent, given attempts to maintain the 'mirror principle' (domestic legislation to mirror ECtHR jurisprudence where possible). The duty of the UK courts is to keep pace with the ECtHR jurisprudence.[39]

Section 3 of HRA 1998 requires legislation to be read and given effect, so far as possible, compatible with rights under the Convention. It applies to primary and subordinate legislation.[40] The obligation to read legislation in this way is mandatory.[41] It does not rely on ambiguity in the underlying legislation.[42] The precise way in which this power should be exercised will vary from case to case.[43]

In considering whether to apply s3 HRA 1999, a court can and must address Parliament's intention as discerned from its enactment of, or decision not to enact, other legislation.[44] The court should adopt a meaning consistent with the fundamental features of the legislation being construed.[45] It is not possible to do violence to the language so as to make it workable,[46] or to commit judicial vandalism by giving the provision an effect quite different from what Parliament intended.[47] A court must not cross the boundary between the interpretation and amendment of legislation.[48]

Applying these principles, in the employment case of *Jessemey v Rowstock*, the Court of Appeal considered whether the "flexible interpretive approach" required under the Convention required domestic law to protect employees from victimisation after dismissal. The Court found that such protection should be available, although, on the face of the decision, the outcome was at some distance from the plain words of the statute.[49]

38 *R v Secretary of State for the Home Department, ex parte Simms* (2000) 2 AC 115, 131.

39 *R (Ullah) v Special Adjudicator* (2004) 2 AC 323; (2004) 3 All ER 785.

40 Section 3(2)(a), thereby removing the doctrine of implied repeal and preventing arguments that subsequent legislation, which was contradictory with the Act, had impliedly repealed it.

41 *Ghaidan v Godin-Mendoza* [2004] UKHL 30, para 59.

42 *Ghaidan*, para 29.

43 *Ghaidan*, para 124.

44 *R (Nicklinson) v Ministry of Justice* [2014] UKSC 38, para 231.

45 *R v Secretary of State for the Home Department ex parte Anderson* [2002] UKHL 46, para 59; *R v Lambert* [2001] UKHL 37, para 79.

46 *Lambert*, para 80.

47 *Anderson*, para 70.

48 *R v Lambert* [2001] UKHL 37, para 79.

49 *Jessemey v Rowstock Ltd and Anor* [2014] EWCA Civ 185, para 25.

Section 4 of the Human Rights Act permits higher courts to make a declaration of incompatibility with respect to the legislation.[50] When a court considers whether to make a declaration of incompatibility, the Crown is entitled to notice of the hearing.[51]

Neither the Employment Tribunal nor the Employment Appeal Tribunal has the power to make a declaration of incompatibility.[52] Once a provision of legislation has been declared incompatible, a minister may, by order, make such amendments to the legislation as they consider necessary to remove the incompatibility.[53]

Section 6 of the Human Rights Act provides that it is unlawful for a public authority to act in a way which is incompatible with a Convention right. This duty applies to courts, as well as other public bodies. The Convention rights within the meaning of the Human Rights Act are, therefore, domestic and not international rights, although the domestic rights so created are expressed in the same terms as those contained in the Convention. Put another way, their formal source is the HRA itself, not the Convention.

Convention rights are understood to be applicable vertically, i.e., individual/group against public authority, but also applicable horizontally, i.e., between individuals. This is because the court, as a public body, has a duty to ensure its judgments do not go against the Convention rights of other individuals. In reliance on this principle, the Court of Appeal held in the employment cases of *X v Y* that courts should determine individual employment cases on the basis that the duty to apply the Convention was relevant to cases against private employers as well as public ones.[54]

Proportionality – general principles

As a matter of domestic law, the general approach to proportionality is as follows. Once a court has found that a person's human rights have been infringed, the Court must then consider the following further matters:

(a) is the legislative objective (legitimate aim) sufficiently important to justify limiting a fundamental right;
(b) are the measures which have been designed to meet it rationally connected to it;
(c) are there no more than are necessary to accomplish it; and

50 Section 4 applies to primary legislation. The Court's powers to declare secondary legislation invalid were considered in *R (Public Law Project) v Lord Chancellor* [2016] UKSC 39, paras 20–3.

51 Human Rights Act 1998, section 5.

52 *Younas v Chief Constable of the Thames Valley Police* [2000] EAT 795/00, para 15.

53 Schedule 2 Human Rights Act 1998.

54 *X v Y* [2004] EWCA Civ 662, para 64. And see Chapter 2.

(d) do they strike a fair balance between the rights of the individual and the interests of the community?[55]

In the *Carlile* case, the Supreme Court upheld the Secretary of State's decision to exclude Mrs Rajavi, an Iranian dissident, from the United Kingdom so that she was unable to accept an invitation to speak to Parliamentarians about issues of human rights and democracy in Iran. Lord Sumption held:

> Even where, as here, the relevant decision maker has carried out the balancing exercise, and has not made any errors of primary fact or principle and has not reached an irrational conclusion, so that the only issue is the proportionality of the decision, the court cannot simply frank the decision, but it must give the decision appropriate weight, and that weight may be decisive.[56]

Interaction with the rights of others

The exercise of the right to freedom of expression also brings certain "responsibilities":

> Amongst them – in the context of religious opinions and beliefs – may legitimately be included an obligation to avoid as far as possible expressions that are gratuitously offensive to others and thus an infringement of their rights, and which therefore do not contribute to any form of public debate capable of furthering progress in human affairs.[57]

It has sometimes been said that article 10 comprises a right not to be insulted or distressed. So, in *Butler v Derby City Council*, the High Court considered a claim for the judicial review of advertising regulations which prohibited a person from hanging a banner opposing the council's plans for road building. Rejecting the idea that the Claimant had any right to display that banner, Sullivan J held:

> There is no absolute right to impart one's views, political or otherwise, in such a way as to amount, for example, to a noise nuisance. Visual intrusion may, in certain circumstances, be no less harmful to the rights of others.[58]

55 *R (Aguilar Quila) v Secretary of State for the Home Department* [2011] UKSC 45, para 45; *Bank Mellatt v HM Treasury (No 2)* [2014] AC 700, paras 68–76.

56 *R (Lord Carlile of Berriew) v Secretary of State for the Home Department* [2014] UKSC 60 para 68.

57 *Giniewski v France* (2007) 45 EHRR 23, para 43.

58 *Butler v Derby City Council* [2005] EWHC 2835, para 38.

Similarly, in proceedings relating to a play which was causing distress to members of the Sikh community, the High Court was less concerned with the legality of an order prohibiting anti-social behaviour in the play's vicinity and more with what they characterised as unlawful behaviour by protesters. In the words of Lady Justice Hallett:

> [With the right to protest] come duties and responsibilities, primarily the duty to respect others' rights. However deeply someone may feel about his religion or a particular cause, if he wishes to protest, he must do so peacefully and lawfully.[59]

Article 14

The principle of non-discrimination is set out in article 14 ECHR:

> The enjoyment of the rights and freedoms set forth in the European Convention on Human Rights and the Human Rights Act shall be secured without discrimination on any ground such as sex, race, colour, language, religion, political or other opinion, national or social origin, association with a national minority, property, birth or other status.

Article 14 does not limit the grounds of protection to established characteristics such as race and sex but to "or other status". A court may, in principle, apply this phrase to any ground for adverse treatment of a group or a class of people that lacks an objective and reasonable justification. So, for example, in *T v Ministry of Defence*, a Tribunal found that rules preventing former servicemen and women from bringing Tribunal claims were contrary to the Convention and unlawful.[60]

Examples of statuses which have been treated by the European Court of Human Rights as protected under the Convention (and which are wider than those set out in Part 4 Equality Act) include prisoners,[61] members of a trade union,[62] freemasons,[63] people defined not by the country of their origins but the country in which they live,[64] and homeowners with a smaller plot of land attached rather than a larger one.[65] Under article 14, protected status includes being the parent of a disabled child.[66]

59 *Singh, R (on the application of) v Chief Constable of West Midlands Police* [2006] EWCA Civ 1118, paras 73–4.
60 *T v Ministry of Defence* [2021] ET claim 2201755/2021.
61 *Stummer v Austria* [2011] ECHR 1096, paras 3, 86.
62 *Danilenkov v Russia* [2009] ECHR 1243, para 136.
63 *Grande Oriente d'Italia di Palazzo Giustiniani v Italie* [2001] ECHR 500, paras 8, 26.
64 *Carson v United Kingdom* [2010] ECHR 338, paras 70–1.
65 *Chassagnou v France* (1999) 29 EHRR 615, paras 19, 121.
66 *Guberina v Croatia* (2018) 66 EHRR 11 at paras 77–9.

In cases before the UK courts, being a parent with parental responsibility brought a Claimant within article 14,[67] as did being the victim of domestic violence,[68] or being homeless,[69] a judge,[70] or a care leaver.[71]

Article 14 does not present an independent right but rather concerns discrimination with respect to other Convention rights. What that means, in practice, is that a litigant does not bring a case with article 14 alone, but, for example, article 10 paired with article 14 or article 8 paired with article 14.

In *Re P and Others,* Lord Hope has held that cases about discrimination in social policy "will always be appropriate for judicial scrutiny" and that the constitutional responsibility in this area of law resides with the courts:

> The constitutional responsibility in this area of our law resides with the courts. The more contentious the issue is, the greater the risk is that some people will be discriminated against in ways that engage their Convention rights. It is for the courts to see that this does not happen. It is with them that the ultimate safeguard against discrimination rests.[72]

In *R (Carson) v Secretary of State for Work and Pensions*, Lord Nicholls set out the circumstances of how article 14 should be applied:

> [T]he essential question for the court is whether the alleged discrimination, that is, the difference in treatment of which complaint is made, can withstand scrutiny. Sometime the answer to this question will be plain . . . Sometimes, where the position is not so clear, a different approach is called for. Then the court's scrutiny may best be directed at considering whether the differentiation has a legitimate aim and whether the means chosen to achieve the aim is appropriate and not disproportionate.[73]

In *Thlimmenos v Greece*, the ECtHR held that Article 14 is not limited to cases where a state treats people in analogous situations differently. Article 14 "is also violated when States without an objective and reasonable justification fail to treat differently persons whose situations are significantly different".[74]

67 *Francis v Secretary of State for Work and Pensions* [2005] EWCA Civ 1303, paras 28–30.

68 *R (on the application of HA) v Ealing London Borough Council* [2015] EWHC 2375, paras 2, 29.

69 *R (on the application of RJM) v the Secretary of State for Work and Pensions* [2008] UKHL 63, para 44.

70 *Gillham v Ministry of Justice* [2019] UKSC 44, para 34.

71 *R (on the application of YA) v London Borough of Hammersmith and Fulham* [2016] EWHC 1850, para 68.

72 *P and Others, Re* [2008] UKHL 38, para 48.

73 *Carson, R (on the application of) v Secretary of State for Work and Pensions* [2005] UKHL 37, para 3.

74 *Thlimmenos v Greece* (2000) 9 BHRC 12, para 44.

Article 17

Article 17 ECHR provides a further limit, excluding the rights set out in the Convention, where their misuse would lead to the destruction of other people's rights:

> Nothing in this Convention may be interpreted as implying for any State, group or person any right to engage in any activity or perform any act aimed at the destruction of any of the rights and freedoms set forth herein or at their limitation to a greater extent than is provided for in the Convention.

To come within article 17, a mere willingness to destroy the rights of others is not sufficient. That desire to negate other people's rights must take the form of an action, including a speech act, which deprives the group or person of their own right to speak:

> In *Levickas v Lithuania*, gay men had been the victims of homophobic language. They suffered threats on Facebook, to "burn in hell", be castrated, burned or "cured[d]", which the state had failed to investigate or restrict. The victims complained that the state had failed to protect their rights under Article 14, and argued that the words of their abusers came within article 17. The ECtHR agreed.[75] The perpetrators had "perform[ed]" linguistic violence against the complainants. The Lithuanian state had unlawfully ignored their complaints.
>
> In *Norwood v United Kingdom*, a member of a far-right British political party displayed a poster representing the Twin Towers in flames and carrying the words "Islam out of Britain – Protect the British People". The message of the poster was British Muslims endangered other people and that their rights should be destroyed. Mr Norwood was prosecuted and convicted of displaying a sign with hostility towards a racial or religious group and received a fine. The ECtHR held that article 17 applied to his case. The decision to prosecute him had infringed his right to free expression, but that infringement had been lawful.[76]

The case law distinguishes three bands of expression by the extent to which they endanger other people's rights. Band (i) is the "gravest" category of language, which clearly stirs up hatred or violence or performs acts aimed at the destruction of the rights and freedom of others and which clearly engages article 17. Band (ii) is a "less grave" category of expression, which

75 *Levickas v Lithuania* [2020] ECHR 19, para 10; also *Sabalić v Croatia* [2021] ECHR 19.

76 *Norwood v United Kingdom* [2004] EHRR 11.

arguably engages article 17 and requires "an assessment of content of the expression and the manner of its delivery". This category will include some language which slanders or is prejudicial or offensive to groups protected by Article 14. Band (iii) covers the majority of language, which does not come close to calling for the destruction of others' rights.[77] Language within band (i) clearly infringers article 17, it cannot be justified, and it loses the protection of freedom of expression. Words within band (iii) are clearly lawful. When expression comes within the intermediate category of band (ii), its legality or otherwise will depend on the context, i.e., what was said and whether the words were bad that they were likely to be felt by their victim as prejudicial or offensive.[78]

Specific limitations on freedom of expression: criminal law

Examples of behaviour which is criminal and, therefore, likely to justify an infringement of article 10 include making threats to kill[79] or speaking or acting in a way that indicates a willingness to use unlawful violence against another person.[80]

Sections 4, 4A, and 5 Public Order Act 1986 prohibit the causing of harassment, alarm, or distress. Section 4A applies to intentional harassment. Section 5 provides that:

> A person is guilty of an offence if he –
>
> (a) uses threatening words or behaviour, or disorderly behaviour, or
> (b) displays any writing, sign or other visible representation which is threatening or abusive, within the hearing or sight of a person likely to be caused harassment, alarm or distress thereby.

Sections 18–23 of the Public Order Act 1986 create various racial hatred offences, including, at section 18, using threatening, abusive, or insulting words or behaviour with the intention or likelihood of stirring up racial hatred.

Sections 29A-F Public Order Act outlaws various offences of hatred against persons on religious grounds.

Section 66 of the Sentencing Act 2020 requires courts to impose aggravated sentences for offences aggravated by racial hostility, religious hostility,

77 *Lilliendahl v Iceland*, application no 29297/18, paras 25–36.
78 *Lilliendahl*, paras 25–36.
79 Section 16 Offences Against the Person Act 1861.
80 Section 39 Criminal Justice Act 1988.

hostility related to disability, hostility related to sexual orientation, or hostility related to transgender identity.

A number of criminal laws prohibit expression which promotes terrorism. For example, Section 2 of the Terrorism Act 2006 prohibits the dissemination of terrorist publications.[81]

A course of conduct of harassment is prohibited by the Protection from Harassment Act 1997.[82]

It is an offence under section 1 of the Computer Misuse Act 1990 to use a computer to access a programme or data without the owner's (or, as may be, the employer)'s authorisation. Amongst other things, this criminal offence, prohibits reading or stealing confidential data, as well as the sending of malicious communications.

Section 1 of the Malicious Communications Act 1988 prohibits the sending of letters or electronic or other communications which are indecent, grossly offensive, or a threat, or contain information which the sender knows to be false.

Section 127 of the Communication Act 2003 outlaws the use of electronic communications networks for improper purposes, meaning communications which are grossly offensive, indecent, obscene, or menacing, or (if the communications are persistent) which contain information which the sender knows to be false.

Some criminal offences are aimed not so much towards the communication of unlawful speech but of acts to intercept or forestall such speech unlawfully. Sections 3–10 of the Investigatory Powers Act 2016 outlaw the unlawful interception of communication.[83]

81 On appeal, the Court of Appeal upheld convictions under that Act, finding that there was no contradiction between them and freedom of expression *R v Ali* [2018] EWCA Crim 547, para 21.

82 Unlike the Public Order Act, the PHA is also capable of enforcement in the civil courts (section 1 PHA 1997). An employer may be vicariously liable for harassment committed by an employee in the course of their employment (*Majrowski v Guy's and St Thomas' NHS Trust* [2006] UKHL 34). Not all behaviour will be so bad as to qualify as harassment under the 1997 Act. In the civil case of *Dowson and Ors v Chief Constable of Northumbria Police* [2010] EWHC 2612, behaviour which was "insensitive, belittling and overbearing" was found not to constitute harassment where its victims were police officers who were used to dealing in their day-to-day working lives "with career-hardened criminals" (paras 277–8). By contrast, in *Veakins v Kier Islington Ltd* [2009] EWCA Civ 1288, the Court of Appeal found that behaviour which reduced a "usually robust woman to a state of clinical depression" was sufficiently bad to come within the Act (para 15).

83 Regulations made under the Act permit monitoring or keeping a record of communications for purposes including "in order to establish the existence of facts" Reg 3, Investigatory Powers (Interception by Businesses, etc., for Monitoring and Record-keeping Purposes) Regulations 2018. To come within this protection the employer must, amongst other things, make all reasonable efforts to inform every person who may use the telecommunication system that communications may be intercepted. Reg 4, Investigatory Powers Regulations.

Other specific limitations on freedom of expression: prevent

Other potential restrictions on freedom of expression are set out in the Equality Act 2010 (these are explored in the next chapter) and in the Prevent Duty.

Section 26 of the Counter-Terrorism and Security Act 2015 requires specified authorities in England, Wales, and Scotland to have "due regard to the need to prevent people from being drawn into terrorism". Guidance published under the duty provides that, for all specified authorities, the government expects those in leadership positions to establish mechanisms for understanding the risk of radicalisation, ensure staff understand the risk and build the capabilities to deal with it, communicate and promote the importance of the duty, and ensure staff implements the duty effectively. The guidance also sets out sector-specific duties for local authorities, schools and registered childcare providers, further and higher education, the health sector, prisons and probation, and the police.[84]

In response to a judicial review brought by a frequent guest speaker on university campuses, Mr Butt, the Court of Appeal struck down in 2019 guidance from the Home Office (the "Higher Education Prevent Duty Guidance") which gave more weight to the need to prevent extremism than the need to protect freedom of expression. The Court held that employers and those advising them needed to be "sufficiently balanced", in their application of "competing obligations"[85] – i.e., they should do all they could in reality, both to allow freedom of expression and to prevent speech which would be criminal.

84 *Revised Prevent Duty Guidance: For England and Wales*, 1 April 2021.

85 *Butt, R (on the application of) v the Secretary of State for the Home Department* [2019] EWCA Civ 256, para 177.

2 Employee protections

Unfair dismissal, equality law, other detriments

While there is no general rule requiring employers to treat their employees reasonably,[1] certain statutory torts do have the effect of limiting how far an employer can go in arbitrarily dismissing an employee or subjecting them to a detriment. The chapter addresses (i) unfair dismissal, (ii) discrimination contrary to the Equality Act 2010, and (iii) other forms of detriment or dismissal which shadow these two main torts. In each case, the discussion begins by explaining how those rights and protections work in general before giving examples of their use in disputes concerning freedom of expression.

Unfair dismissal

Under the Employment Rights Act 1996, an employer may not unfairly dismiss their employee.[2] A dismissal may only be fair if it is for one of a limited number of potentially fair reasons (conduct, capability, retirement, redundancy, an inability to work without contravention of a legal duty, or some other substantial reason). The burden is on the employer to prove the reason for the dismissal.[3]

Suppose that an employee has privately expressed the opinion that the world is flat and has done so in a way that has caused no conceivable harm to the employer. Where the employer dismisses that employee, the dismissal may well be unlawful as it is contrary to the Equality Act 2010, which protects opinions and beliefs (see further on). However, even without needing to invoke the Equality Act, such a dismissal would, on its face, be arbitrary and capricious. Since the employee has been dismissed for a reason which is not one of the limited reasons permitted under the Act, the dismissal would be unfair and, therefore, unlawful. The employee would, in principle, be entitled to the protections afforded by the Act, including compensation for dismissal[4] and reinstatement or re-engagement.[5]

1 *Post Office v Roberts* [1980] IRLR 347.
2 Section 94 Employment Rights Act 1996.
3 Section 98 Employment Rights Act 1996.
4 Section 118 Employment Rights Act 1996.
5 Sections 114 and 115 Employment Rights Act 1996.

DOI: 10.4324/9781032724263-2

Section 98 Employment Rights Act 1996 provides that it is for the employer to show the reason for a dismissal and that such a reason is a potentially fair reason. A reason for the dismissal of an employee is "a set of fact known to the employer, or it may be of beliefs held by him, which cause him to dismiss the employee".[6]

It is open to the Tribunal to find that there was a real reason for the dismissal, which was a different reason to the one given by the employer, in which case it may substitute the correct reason provided that the necessary facts have been established.[7] The burden is on the employer to satisfy the Tribunal that the reason it relied upon was indeed the true reason.[8]

Although different tests apply to each of the statutory reasons for dismissal, in broad terms, any dismissal must be within the range of reasonable responses which a reasonable employer might take.[9] That test shields the employer's reasoning: a Tribunal must not substitute its own view of what should have happened for the view of the employer. Whether or not the employer's decision to dismiss falls within the range of reasonable responses depends on the employer's knowledge at the time the decision was taken.[10]

Where the employer has committed a fundamental breach of contract, the employee is entitled to treat the employment contract as being at an end by terminating their employment forthwith.[11] The contract does not automatically end; to give effect to this right, the employee must take the initiative and resign.

Inter-relationship of freedom of expression and unfair dismissal

In an unfair dismissal case in which an employee's Convention rights are engaged, the appropriate procedure is as follows. The ET has no jurisdiction to entertain a claim for a breach of a Claimant's rights under the ECHR as such.[12] However, under section 3 of the Human Rights Act, an Employment Tribunal, so far as it is possible to do so, must read and give effect to the relevant provisions of the applicable statute (here section 98 Employment Rights Act 1996) in a way which is compatible with Convention rights,[13] including article 10 which protects freedom of expression.

An important case which engaged an employee's Convention rights was *X v Y*, which was heard in the Court of Appeal in 2004 with Mummery LJ

6 *Abernethy v Mott Hay and Anderson* [1974] ICR 323, 330.
7 *W Devis and Sons Ltd v Atkins* [1977] AC 931.
8 *Maund v Penwith District Council* [1984] ICR 143.
9 *Iceland Frozen Foods v Jones* [1982] ICR 17, 24.
10 *Asda Stores Ltd v Malyn* (2001) 3 WLUK 134, para 18.
11 *Western Excavating v Sharp* [1978] IRLR 27.
12 *Mba v Mertong London Borough Council* [2014] ICR 357.
13 *Page v NHS Trust Development Authority* [2021] EWCA Civ 255, para 37.

presiding. The employee, who worked with young offenders, had accepted a caution after committing a sex offence with another man in a lavatory. The Appellant was dismissed for gross misconduct. The Court gave guidance as to the procedure which should be followed in cases where an employee's Convention rights were engaged. The Tribunal should ask:

(1) Do the circumstances of the dismissal fall within the ambit of one or more of the articles of the Convention? If they do not, the Convention right is not engaged and need not be considered.
(2) If they do, does the state have a positive obligation to secure enjoyment of the relevant Convention right between private persons? If it does not, the Convention right is unlikely to affect the outcome of an unfair dismissal claim against a private employer.
(3) If it does, is the interference with the employee's Convention right by dismissal justified? If it is, proceed to (5).
(4) If it is not, was there a permissible reason for the dismissal under the ERA, which does not involve unjustified interference with a Convention right? If there was not, the dismissal will be unfair for the absence of a permissible reason to justify it.
(5) If there was, is the dismissal fair, tested by the provisions of section 98 of the ERA, reading and giving effect to them under section 3 of the HRA so as to be compatible with the Convention right?[14]

Equality Act

Discrimination against nine protected characteristics is prohibited under the Equality Act 2010. These are age, disability, gender reassignment, marriage and civil partnership, pregnancy and maternity, race, religion or belief, sex, and sexual orientation (section 4 Equality Act 2010). The Act prohibits various forms of discrimination, including direct discrimination (section 13 EA 2010), indirect discrimination (section 19 EA 210), harassment (section 26 EA 2010), and victimisation (section 27 EA 2010).

Direct discrimination

Direct discrimination takes place when:

> A person (A) discriminates against another (B) if, because of a protected characteristic, A treats B less favourably than A treats or would treat others.[15]

14 *X v Y* [2004] EWCA Civ 662, para 64.
15 Section 13 Equality Act 2010.

At the heart of direct discrimination is the idea of comparison: a black person or a woman had been treated less favourably in circumstances where a white person or a man was treated, or would have been treated, more favourably.

For many years, it was believed that the most effective way in which to prove direct discrimination was through the creation of "comparators", actual or hypothetical people whose differential treatment proved the discrimination. So that, if, for example, a black person acting in a certain way in the workplace received a detriment, perhaps a warning, and a white person acting in the same way received no detriment, this was cogent evidence from which the Tribunal could infer that race was the reason for the detriment.

A core difficulty with this method became apparent in that a judge could not know how an imaginary person – the hypothetical comparator – would be treated.

In *Shamoon v Chief Constable of the Royal Ulster Constabulary*, Lord Nicholls pointed out that the identification of a hypothetical comparator was artificial, often meaningless, and usually was the wrong question to ask. Before being able to answer whether the correct hypothetical comparator had been identified or how they would have been treated, the Court first needed to know why a Claimant had been treated a certain way, and it was this "reason why" question which provided the real answer to discrimination claims.[16]

Since *Shamoon*, the approach has been to reject the search for comparators in favour of asking, in as simple a way as possible, why particular behaviour occurred.[17]

In deciding whether a person has suffered less favourable treatment, the question to be asked is whether the treatment of such a kind that a reasonable employee would or might take the view that, in all the circumstances, it was to their detriment. It is not necessary for a Claimant to show financial loss.[18] In *Omooba v Michael Garrett Associates*, an actor was dismissed from a potential role before it started. The actor later confirmed that, in any event, she would not have taken the role. The Tribunal found, however, that the Claimant had "experienced some hurt at being dropped", and this was sufficient to be capable of constituting detriment, notwithstanding that there was no objective loss.[19]

At the core of direct discrimination is the idea of less favourable treatment because of a protected characteristic. This is a question of causation.

16 *Shamoon v Chief Constable of the RUC* [2003] ICR 337, paras 10–11.

17 *Page v NHS Trust Development Authority* [2021] EWCA Civ 255, para 79: "It is *not* necessary in every case to construct a hypothetical comparator, and that doing so is often a less straightforward route to the right result than making a finding as to the reason why the respondent did the act complained of".

18 *Shamoon*, para 35.

19 *Omooba v Michael Garrett Associates Ltd & Anor* [2024] EAT 30, paras 148–51.

The Tribunal must focus on the mind of the decision maker responsible for the detriment relied on by the Claimant.

One limited exception to the focus on the decision-makers applies, in whistleblowing cases only,[20] where a person in the hierarchy of responsibility above the dismissing officer determines that the employee should be dismissed and that the reason should be hidden behind an invented reason, which the decision maker adopts. In those circumstances, it is the Court's duty to establish the real reason for dismissal.[21]

Where there are two decision-makers reaching their decision jointly, to succeed in a claim, a Claimant only needs to show that one was acting on discriminatory motivation.[22]

In order for a person to suffer discrimination, there is no requirement that the perpetrator must have accurately identified that the victim belonged to one of the categories protected by the Equality Act. Discrimination is made if a person is the victim of unwanted conduct on account of characteristics which are merely associated with a protected ground. So, in *English v Thomas Sanderson Blinds*,[23] a group of employees subjected a straight colleague to sexual innuendo to the effect that he was gay, teasing him on account of the fact that he lived in Brighton and had attended boarding school, facts which in the minds of his discriminators could have shown that he was gay.

In *Chief Constable of Norfolk v Coffey*, a police officer with a hearing impairment was similarly protected from discrimination grounds of that impairment, notwithstanding that the impairment was insufficiently serious to make them disabled.[24]

Where A discriminates against B because of a protected characteristic belonging to a different person C, that, too, is unlawful. So, for example, in *Showboat Entertainment Centre Ltd v Owens*,[25] a white employee was dismissed for refusing to carry out an instruction from his employers to exclude black youths from an entertainment centre. That instruction was unlawful, even though both A and B had the same racial heritage, and the discriminatory malice was directed at another person.

In all direct discrimination complaints, with the sole exception of age, there is no justification defence.

Section 158 and 159 to the Equality Act 2010 permits employers to take positive action both in general and specifically in relation to recruitment and promotion where persons who share a protected characteristic suffer a

20 *Alcedo Orange Ltd v Ferridge-Gunn* [2023] EAT 78, para 32.

21 *Royal Mail Group v Jhuti* [2020] ICR 731.

22 *CLFIS (UK) Ltd v Reynolds* [2015] EWCA Civ 439, para 32; *The Commissioner of Police of the Metropolis v Denby* [2017] EAT 0314/16.

23 *English v Thomas Sanderson Blinds Ltd* [2009] IRLR 206, para 69.

24 *Chief Constable of Norfolk v Coffey* [2019] EWCA Civ 1061, para 74.

25 *Showboat Entertainment Centre Ltd v Owens* [1984] ICR 65, 73.

disadvantage connected to the characteristic or participation in an activity by persons who share a protected characteristic is disproportionately low. The conceptual importance of this provision is that it operates as a counterweight to what would otherwise be the prohibition on direct discrimination. Absent section 159, a woman's organisation offering services to domestic violence, for example, could not advertise a service asking for a female candidate since to do so would directly discriminate against any men interested in that post.

Indirect discrimination

Indirect discrimination takes place when a person (A) applies to another person (B) a provision, criterion, or practice which is discriminatory in relation to a relevant protected characteristic of theirs. The act is indirectly discriminatory if:

(a) A applies, or would apply, it to persons with whom B does not share the characteristic,
(b) it puts, or would put, persons with whom B shares the characteristic at a particular disadvantage when compared with persons with whom B does not share it,
(c) it puts, or would put, B at that disadvantage, and
(d) A cannot show it to be a proportionate means of achieving a legitimate aim.[26]

A key question in indirect discrimination cases is: what is the provision, criterion, or practice which is said to have the discriminatory effect? A mere one-off failure to follow a written policy is not a "practice".[27]

In *Pendleton v Derbyshire County Council*, a school dismissed a teacher after she elected to remain with her husband after he had been convicted of making indecent images of children and voyeurism. The school demanded a certain conduct (i.e., expression) from the teacher; it expected her to end her relationship with him publicly, but this she refused to do. The Tribunal held that the relevant provision, criterion, or practice was a policy to dismiss those who choose not to end a relationship with a person convicted of making indecent images of children and voyeurism. While such a policy was, on its surface, neutral, it was likely to cause disadvantage to people like the Claimant, who was a committed and practising Anglican Christian, and it was not proportionate since the Respondents had failed to show that such a policy would protect or safeguard schoolchildren. The EAT held that where there is a policy or a management decision, it is capable of qualifying as a

26 Section 19 Equality Act 2010.

27 *Nottingham City Transport Ltd v Harvey* EAT 0032/12, para 18.

provision, criterion, or practice, even if that policy or practice will only be rarely applied.[28]

As with detriments in direct discrimination, the Claimant is required to show disadvantage. Unlike direct discrimination, there is no need to show any causative link between the PCP and the detriment; it is enough that the Claimant suffers disadvantage.[29]

In an indirect discrimination claim, where the employer pleads justification, the following principles apply:[30]

(1) The burden of proof is on the respondent to establish justification.[31]
(2) The classic test was set out in *Bilka-Kaufhas GmbH v Weber Von Hartz* in the context of indirect sex discrimination. The ECJ said that the Court or Tribunal must be satisfied that the measures must "correspond to a real need . . . are appropriate with a view to achieving the objectives pursued and are necessary to that end"[32] . . . The reference to "necessary" means "reasonably necessary."[33]
(3) The principle of proportionality requires an objective balance to be struck between the discriminatory effect of the measure and the needs of the undertaking. The more serious the disparate adverse impact, the more cogent the justification for it must be.[34]
(4) It is for the employment tribunal to weigh the reasonable needs of the undertaking against the discriminatory effect of the employer's measure and to make its own assessment of whether the former outweighs the latter. There is no 'range of reasonable response' test in this context.[35]

Harassment

The most important of the statutory torts, in the context of freedom of expression, is the prohibition on harassment. That act is defined by section 26(1) EA 2010 as follows:

> A person (A) harasses another (B) if –
>
> (a) A engages in unwanted conduct related to a relevant protected characteristic and

28 *Pendleton v Derbyshire County Council and Anor* [2016] EAT 0238/15, para 35.
29 *Essop v Home Office* [2017] UKSC 27, paras 31–3.
30 *MacCulloch v Imperial Chemical Industries plc* [2008] EAT 0119/08, para 10.
31 *Starmer v British Airways* [2005] IRLR 863, para 31.
32 *Bilka-Kaufhas GmbH v Weber Von Hartz* [1984] IRLR 317, para 36.
33 *Rainey v Greater Glasgow Health Board* [1987] ICR 129, 142–3.
34 *Hardys and Hansons plc v Lax* [2005] IRLR 726, paras 19–34, 54–5, 60.
35 *Hardys and Hansons plc v Lax*.

(b) the conduct has the purpose or effect of –

(i) violating B's dignity, or
(ii) creating an intimidating, hostile, degrading, humiliating, or offensive environment for B.

The formal separation of purpose and effect, and the possibility that a Claimant may succeed on either limb has further consequences which are not straightforward. It means, for example that a Respondent may be held liable on the basis that the effect of the conduct has been to produce the proscribed consequences even if that was not its purpose and, conversely, that a Respondent may be liable if they acted for the purposes of producing the proscribed consequences but did not in fact do so.[36]

Sub-section (4) of section 26 provides that in deciding whether the conduct was so bad as to amount to harassment, the subjective feelings of the victim are a significant but not necessarily decisive consideration:

> In deciding whether conduct has the effect referred to in subsection (1)(b), each of the following must be taken into account –
>
> (a) the perception of B;
> (b) the other circumstances of the case;
> (c) whether it is reasonable for the conduct to have that effect.

In other words, when a Tribunal decides whether behaviour was bad enough to be harassment, the Tribunal should take into account the personal characteristics of the victim (for example, if there was anything about their private history which made them particularly susceptible to being upset by harassment), and their subjective reaction to it, but there is in the final resort a threshold of objective seriousness, so that behaviour may be unwanted or unpleasant but not so bad as to violate a person's dignity.[37]

In *Heafield v Times Newspaper Ltd*, a newsroom editor shouted at a room of executives, "Can anyone tell what's happening to the fucking Pope?". The editor did not have any malicious intent; he simply wanted the article about the Pope and used bad language because he was under pressure. The EAT held that:

> [N]ot every racially slanted adverse comment or conduct may constitute the violation of a person's dignity. Dignity is not necessarily violated by things said or done which are trivial or transitory.[38]

36 *Richmond Pharmaceuticals v Dhaliwal* [2009] ICR 724, para 14.
37 *Richmond Pharmaceuticals*, para 15.
38 *Heafield v Times Newspaper Ltd* [2013] EAT 1305/12, paras 2, 9–10; *Richmond Pharmaceuticals*, para 22.

In civil cases, it has been found that the prohibition against harassment does not give members of the public a right to sue for statements published in the press or online where they are directed at the public at large.[39]

Victimisation

Section 27 Equality Act 2010 provides:

(1) A person (A) victimises another person (B) if A subjects B to a detriment because –

  (a) B does a protected act, or
  (b) A believes that B has done, or may do, a protected act.

(2) Each of the following is a protected act –

  (a) bringing proceedings under this Act;
  (b) giving evidence or information in connection with proceedings under this Act;
  (c) doing any other thing for the purposes of or in connection with this Act;
  (d) making an allegation (whether or not expressed) that A or another person has contravened this Act.

(3) Giving false evidence or information or making a false allegation is not a protected act if the evidence or information is given or the allegation is made in bad faith.

Victimisation protects those who exercise a right under the Act or help others to do so. Its aim is to make the remedies available under the Act by ensuring that those who suffer detriment or less favourable treatment are not intimidated from asserting those rights.

The analysis of causation is conducted in a like way to direct discrimination by asking what *the reason why* the detrimental act occurred.

Burden of proof

Section 136 Equality Act 2010 establishes a two-stage process for analysing complaints of discrimination. At the first stage, the Tribunal must ask itself if the Claimant has proved facts, on the balance of probabilities, from which the Tribunal could conclude, in the absence of an adequate explanation, that an

39 *Sube and Anor v News Group Newspapers Ltd and Anor* [2018] EWHC 1234, paras 82–4. Similar considerations apply to libels published in relation to large or indeterminate groups of people. *Knupffer v London Express Newspapers Ltd* [1944] AC 116, at 122.

unlawful act of discrimination has been committed. Mere differential treatment is not enough to make the burden shift.[40]

If a Claimant has proved such facts, the burden moves to the employer to explain the reason(s) for the treatment and satisfy the Tribunal that the protected characteristic played no part in those reasons. Unless the employer discharges that burden, the claim succeeds.

The reason for placing the burden on the employer at the second stage is that the knowledge of the reasons for the conduct is the employer's. As Lord Browne-Wilkinson observed in *Glasgow City Council v Zafar*: "those who discriminate . . . do not in general advertise their prejudices: indeed, they may not even be aware of them".[41]

In the guideline case of *Igen Ltd and Ors v Wong*, the Court of Appeal held that the way to apply section 136 was as follows:

> Pursuant to section 63A of the SDA,[42] it is for the claimant who complains of sex discrimination to prove on the balance of probabilities facts from which the tribunal could conclude, in the absence of an adequate explanation, that the respondent has committed an act of discrimination against the claimant which is unlawful by virtue of Part II or which by virtue of s. 41 or s. 42 of the SDA[43] is to be treated as having been committed against the claimant. These are referred to below as "such facts".
>
> If the claimant does not prove such facts he or she will fail.
>
> It is important to bear in mind in deciding whether the claimant has proved such facts that it is unusual to find direct evidence of sex discrimination. Few employers would be prepared to admit such discrimination, even to themselves. In some cases, the discrimination will not be an intention but merely based on the assumption that "he or she would not have fitted in".
>
> In deciding whether the claimant has proved such facts, it is important to remember that the outcome at this stage of the analysis by the tribunal will therefore usually depend on what inferences it is proper to draw from the primary facts found by the tribunal.
>
> It is important to note the word "could" in s. 63A(2). At this stage the tribunal does not have to reach a definitive determination that such facts would lead it to the conclusion that there was an act of unlawful discrimination. At this stage a tribunal is looking at the primary facts before it to see what inferences of secondary fact could be drawn from them.
>
> In considering what inferences or conclusions can be drawn from the primary facts, the tribunal must assume that there is no adequate explanation for those facts.

40 *Birmingham City Council Millwood* [2012] EAT/0564, para 29.
41 *Glasgow City Council v Zafar* [1997] 1 WLR 1659 at 1664.
42 The relevant statutory provision is now section 136 Equality Act 2010.
43 Now sections 109 and 112 Equality Act 2010.

These inferences can include, in appropriate cases, any inferences that it is just and equitable to draw in accordance with section 74(2)(b) of the SDA from an evasive or equivocal reply to a questionnaire or any other questions that fall within section 74(2) of the SDA.

Likewise, the tribunal must decide whether any provision of any relevant code of practice is relevant and if so, take it into account in determining, such facts pursuant to section 56A(10) of the SDA. This means that inferences may also be drawn from any failure to comply with any relevant code of practice.

Where the claimant has proved facts from which conclusions could be drawn that the respondent has treated the claimant less favourably on the ground of sex, then the burden of proof moves to the respondent.

It is then for the respondent to prove that he did not commit, or as the case may be, is not to be treated as having committed, that act.

To discharge that burden it is necessary for the respondent to prove, on the balance of probabilities, that the treatment was in no sense whatsoever on the grounds of sex, since "no discrimination whatsoever" is compatible with the Burden of Proof Directive.[44]

That requires a tribunal to assess not merely whether the respondent has proved an explanation for the facts from which such inferences can be drawn, but further that it is adequate to discharge the burden of proof on the balance of probabilities that sex was not a ground for the treatment in question.

Since the facts necessary to prove an explanation would normally be in the possession of the respondent, a tribunal would normally expect cogent evidence to discharge that burden of proof.[45]

Multiple reasons for discriminatory acts

It is common for an employer to have more than one reason for causing an employee a detriment and to combine a reason which is lawful with one which is unlawful. Elias J held in *Law Society v Bahl* that "the discriminatory reason for the conduct need not be the sole or even the principal reason of the discrimination; it is enough that it is a contributing cause in the sense of a significant influence".[46]

In *Nagarajan v London Regional Transport*, it was said that:

> Discrimination may be on racial grounds even though it is not the sole ground for the decision. A variety of phrases, with different shades of meaning, have been used to explain how the legislation applies in such cases:

44 Article 2(1), Council Directive 2000/78/EC of 27 November 2000 Establishing a General Framework for Equal Treatment in Employment and Occupation.

45 *Igen Ltd and Ors v Wong* [2005] EWCA Civ 142, para 76.

46 *Law Society v Bahl* [2003] IRLR 640, para 83.

> discrimination requires that racial grounds were a cause, the activating cause, a substantial and effective cause, a substantial reason, an important factor. No one phrase is obviously preferable to all others, although in the application of this legislation legalistic phrases, as well as subtle distinctions, are better avoided so far as possible. If racial grounds or protected acts had a significant influence on the outcome, discrimination is made out.[47]

In *Efobi v Royal Mail Group Ltd*, the *Nagarajan* test was summarised as follows: "it did not matter if the employer had acted for an unfair or discreditable reason provided that the reason had nothing to do with the protected characteristic".[48]

Employer's liability

Section 109 Equality Act makes employers and principals liable for acts of discrimination, harassment, and victimisation carried out by their employees in the course of employment or by their agents acting under their authority. The section "imposes a form of constructive liability by deeming the employer himself to have committed the act of discrimination as well as the employed person".[49] It does not matter whether or not the employer or principal knows about or approves of those acts.

However, sub-section 109(4) of the same section provides that it is a defence to the employer to show that it took all reasonable steps to prevent the discriminator from acting unlawfully. Where the employer relies on this defence, the Court should follow a three-stage approach: (a) identify any steps that had been taken; (b) consider whether they were reasonable; and (c) consider whether any other steps should reasonably have been taken. If there was a further step that should reasonably have been taken by the employer to prevent harassment, the defence would fail, even if that step would not have prevented the harassment.[50]

Other relevant powers and duties under the Act

Section 149(1) EA 2010 requires public sector bodies to have due regard to the need to:

(a) eliminate discrimination, harassment, victimisation and any other conduct that is prohibited by or under this Act;

47 *Nagarajan v London Regional Transport* [2000] 1 AC 501, 513. In *Igen Ltd v Wong*, Gibson LJ accepted *Nagarajan*, noting that a "significant" influence is only an influence which is more than trivial (para 37).

48 *Efobi v Royal Mail Group Ltd* [2021] UKSC 33, para 28.

49 *Kemeh v Ministry of Defence* [2014] ICR 625, para 10.

50 *Allay v Gehlen* [2021] ICR 645, paras 24–6.

(b) advance equality of opportunity between persons who share a relevant protected characteristic and persons who do not share it;
(c) foster good relations between persons who share a relevant protected characteristic and persons who do not share it.

Section 149(3) EA 2010 provides further matters to which public sector employers must give due regard, including:

(c) encourag[ing] persons who share a relevant protected characteristic to participate in public life or in any other activity in which participation by such persons is disproportionately low.

The public sector equality duty applies to public authorities and those carrying out public functions. The significance of the duty is discussed in Chapter 5.

Religion or belief

The right in UK law to protection in respect of religion or belief was introduced to ensure compliance with EU law, specifically Council Directive 2000/78/EC ("the Framework Directive"). The recitals of the Framework Directive emphasise the fundamental values of liberty, democracy, and of economic and social cohesion. Recital 11 acknowledges that:

> Discrimination based on religion or belief . . . may undermine the achievement of the objectives of the EC Treaty, in particular the attainment of a high level of employment and social protection, raising the standard of living and the quality of life, economic and social cohesion and solidarity, and the free movement of persons.

The protection afforded by the Framework Directive in respect of religion and belief applies not only to the holding of a particular faith or belief but also to its manifestation. So, for example, in *Bougnaoui v Micropole SA*, it was held that:

> In so far as the ECHR and, subsequently, the Charter use the term 'religion' in a broad sense, in that they include in it the freedom of persons to manifest their religion, the EU legislature must be considered to have intended to take the same approach when adopting Directive 2000/78, and therefore the concept of 'religion' in Article 1 of that directive should be interpreted as covering both the *forum internum*, that is the fact of having a belief, and the *forum externum*, that is the manifestation of religious faith in public.[51]

51 *Bougnaoui v Micropole SA* [2018] ICR 139, para 30.

Section 10 of the Equality Act 2010 sets out the statutory definition of religion or belief:

(1) Religion means any religion, and a reference to religion includes a reference to a lack of religion.
(2) Belief means any religious or philosophical belief, and a reference to belief includes a reference to a lack of belief.
(3) In relation to the protected characteristic of religion or belief –

  (a) a reference to a person who has a particular protected characteristic is a reference to a person of a particular religion or belief;
  (b) a reference to persons who share a protected characteristic is a reference to persons who are of the same religion or belief.

Before considering whether a belief amounts to a "philosophical belief" protected under section 10 of the 2010 Act, the Tribunal must define exactly what the belief is.[52] When deciding whether a religion or belief is entitled to be protected under the Act, it is not for the Court to inquire into the validity of the belief.[53]

As for which beliefs are entitled to the protection of the Act, the leading case is *Grainger Plc and Ors v Nicholson*. There, Burton P set out the minimum requirements:[54]

The belief must be genuinely held.

It must be a belief and not, as in *McClintock v Department of Constitutional Affairs*,[55] an opinion or viewpoint based on the present state of information available.

It must be a belief as to a weighty and substantial aspect of human life and behaviour.

It must attain a certain level of cogency, seriousness, cohesion and importance.

It must be worthy of respect in a democratic society, be not incompatible with human dignity and not conflict with the fundamental rights of others (*Campbell v United Kingdom*[56] and *Williamson*).[57]

In *Harron v Chief Constable of Dorset Police* [2016] IRLR 481, the EAT held that, when determining what constitutes a belief qualifying for protection,

52 *Gray v Mulberry Co (Design) Ltd* [2020] ICR 715, para 26.
53 *R (Williamson) v Secretary of State for Education and Employment* (2005) 2 AC 246, para 22.
54 *Grainger Plc and Ors v Nicholson* [2010] IRLR 4, para 24.
55 *McClintock v Department of Constitutional Affairs* [2008] IRLR 29.
56 *Campbell and Cosans v United Kingdom* [1982] 4 EHRR 293, para 36.
57 *R v Secretary of State for Education and Employment ex parte Williamson* [2005] UKHL 15, para 23.

there is no material difference between the domestic approach under the EA 2010 and that under Article 9 of the Convention.[58]

The Grainger criteria were endorsed by Choudhury J in *Gray v Mulberry Company (Design) Ltd* [2019] ICR 175, EAT[1]. In that case, the EAT emphasised that the bar is not set too high in general and especially in relation to the fourth *Grainger* criterion:

> [T]he proper approach to the application of the *Grainger* criteria (and in particular to the fourth *Grainger* criterion) is simply to ensure that the bar is not set too high, and that too much is not demanded, in terms of threshold requirements, of those professing to have philosophical beliefs. The justification for not setting the bar too high is that it is not for the court to judge the validity of a philosophical belief. It was said by Lord Nicholls in *Williamson* that, "Each individual is at liberty to hold his own religious beliefs, however irrational or inconsistent they may seem to some, however surprising". . .[59] [I]n an application of the *Grainger* criteria, and the fourth *Grainger* criterion in particular, the focus should be on the manifestation of the belief.[60]

Examples of the operation of the *Grainger* criteria include that a belief in man-made climate change and the resulting moral imperatives was found by the Employment Appeal Tribunal to be capable, if genuinely held, of being a philosophical belief;[61] so were the ideas of a spiritualist, who believed that that the dead can be contacted through mediums or psychics;[62] so also was the belief in "left-wing democratic socialist" values, including a belief in workers' control of industry;[63] as was the belief in ethical veganism;[64] in participatory democracy;[65] and the belief that the marriage vow was sacrosanct.[66] Other protected beliefs have included religious hostility to Covid vaccines,[67] support for Scottish independence,[68] anti-Zionism,[69] and a belief that homosexuality is sinful.[70]

58 *Harron v Chief Constable of Dorset Police* [2016] IRLR 481.
59 *R v Secretary of State for Education and Employment ex parte Williamson* [2005] UKHL 15, para 22.
60 *Harron v Chief Constable of Dorset Police* [2016] IRLR 481, paras 28–9.
61 *Grainger Plc and Ors v Nicholson* [2010] IRLR 4, para 32.
62 *Greater Manchester Police Authority v Power* [2009] EAT 0434/09.
63 *General Municipal and Boilermakers Union v Henderson* [2015] EAT 0073/14, para 6.
64 *Costa v The League Against Cruel Sports* [2020] ET case no 3331129/2018; *R Mysakowski v Broxburn Bottlers Ltd* [2024] UKET 8000379/2023. However, in another first-instance case, *Owen v Willow Tower Opco 1 Ltd* (2023) 5 WLUK 543, a belief in veganism did not satisfy the *Grainger*-criteria.
65 *Scottish Federation of Housing Associations v Jones* [2022] EAT 114, para 20.
66 *Pendleton v Derbyshire County Council and Anor* [2016] EAT 0238/15.
67 *Wierowska v HC-One Oval Ltd* [2021] ET case no 1403077/2021.
68 *McEleny v Ministry of Defence* [2017] ET case no 4105347/17.
69 *Miller v University of Bristol* [2024] case no 1400780/2022.
70 *Omooba v Michael Garrett Associates Ltd & Anor* [2024] EAT 30.

On the other hand, the belief that "public service broadcasting has the higher purpose of promoting cultural interchange and social cohesion" and that senior managers should subscribe to this ethos was not sufficiently cogent to amount to a protected belief.[71] A belief in the statutory human or moral right to own the copyright and moral rights of her own creative works and output, except when that creative work or output is produced on behalf of an employer, was not protected.[72] Nor was mere vegetarianism,[73] Trotskyism,[74] English nationalism,[75] or the idea that a global elite was seeking to establish a New World Order.[76]

Section 10 has been given effect consistently with Article 9 of the European Convention on Human Rights, which protects the right of people to hold opinions, which it makes absolute ("Everyone has the right to freedom of thought, conscience and religion"). As we have seen in Chapter 1, the same article then makes the manifestation of religious belief a qualified right.

The distinction between an absolute right to hold opinions, and a qualified right to manifest them has shaped a number of domestic cases. So, for example, in *Williamson*, Christian parents and teachers sought to challenge the statutory ban on the use of corporal punishment in schools. The House of Lords found that the interference with the manifestation of the Claimants' beliefs was in accordance with the law and necessary to protect children.[77]

Where claims for discrimination succeed, the primary remedy is a declaration.[78] The Claimant may also be entitled to compensation.

The leading case on quantum discrimination cases is the 2002 decision of *Vento v Chief Constable of West Yorkshire Police*. The Court of Appeal decided that damages in discrimination cases should be awarded as follows:

(1) The top band should normally be between £15,000 and £25,000. Sums in this range should be awarded in the most serious cases, such as where there has been a lengthy campaign of discriminatory harassment on the ground of sex or race. This case falls within that band. Only in the most exceptional case should an award of compensation for injury to feelings exceed £25,000.

71 *Maistry v BBC* [2014] EWCA Civ 1116, paras 3, 13. Also *Harron v Chief Constable of Dorset Police* EAT 0234/15, concerning the belief that public money should not be wasted.

72 *Gray v Mulberry Company (Design) Ltd* [2019] EWCA Civ 1720.

73 *Conisbee v Crossley Farms Ltd and Ors* [2019] ET 3335357/2018, para 44.

74 *Kelly v Unison* [2008] ET case no 2203854/08.

75 *Cave v Open University*, ET case no 3313198/2020; also *Thomas v Surrey and Borders Partnership NHS Foundation Trust and Ms A Brett* [2021] ET case no 2304056/2018, although that decision was under appeal at the time this book was written.

76 *Farrell v South Yorkshire* [2010] ET case no 2803805/10.

77 *R v Secretary of State for Education and Employment ex parte Williamson* [2005] UKHL 15.

78 Section 124 Equality Act 2010.

(2) The middle band of between £5,000 and £15,000 should be used for serious cases, which do not merit an award in the highest band.
(3) Awards of between £500 and £5,000 are appropriate for less serious cases, such as where the act of discrimination is an isolated or one-off occurrence. In general, awards of less than £500 are to be avoided altogether, as they risk being regarded as so low as not to be a proper recognition of injury to feelings.[79]

Since 2002, the amounts set out in Vento have been increased to take into account of both inflation and the general increase in tort damages arising from the decision of the Court of Appeal in *Simmons v Castle*.[80]

Guidance is published annually by the Presidents of the Employment Tribunal in England, Wales, and Scotland (Addendum to Presidential Guidance). The addendum to the Presidential Guidance, published in spring 2024, provided that:

> In respect of claims presented on or after 6 April 2024, the Vento bands shall be as follows: a lower band of £1,200 *to* £11,700 (less serious cases); a middle band of £11,700 *to* £35,200 (cases that do not merit an award in the upper band); and an upper band of £35,200 *to* £58,700 (the most serious cases), with the most exceptional cases capable of exceeding £58,700.[81]

Practitioners are encouraged to consult the latest version of the Addendum to Presidential Guidance before calculating the damages of any claim.

Other statutory torts

Employees are also protected against detriments on several grounds, including (but not limited to) health and safety,[82] trade union activity,[83] taking maternity or parental leave,[84] being summonsed to attend jury service,[85] asserting

79 *Vento v Chief Constable of West Yorkshire Police* [2002] EWCA Civ 1871, para 65.

80 *Simmons v Castle* [2012] EWCA Civ 1039.

81 Presidential Guidance, 'Employment Tribunal Awards for Injury to Feelings and Psychiatric Injury Following *De Souza v Vinci Construction (UK) Ltd* [2017] EWCA Civ 879,' 25 March 2024, para 2.

82 Sections 44 and 100 Employment Rights Act 1996.

83 Section 152 and 156 Trade Union and Labour Relations (Consolidation) Act 1992; *Wilson and Palmer v The United Kingdom* [2002] EHR 2; *Danilenkov v Russia* [2009] ECHR 1243; *Kaya and Seyhan v Turkey*, application no 30946/04.

84 Section 18 Equality Act 2010; regulation 19, The Maternity and Parental Leave etc. Regulations 1999; Regulation 33 Additional Paternity Leave Regulations 2010.

85 Sections 43M and 98B Employment Rights Act 1996.

a statutory right,[86] seeking to enforce laws under part-time worker or agency worker protections,[87] seeking to enforce rights under the working time regulations,[88] making a protected disclosure for the purposes of whistleblowing legislation,[89] etc.

From the perspective of freedom of expression, the most important of these rights is the protection afforded to whistleblowers. To trigger that protection, the employer must have made a qualifying disclosure,[90]

(a) that a criminal offence has been committed, is being committed, or is likely to be committed,
(b) that a person has failed, is failing, or is likely to fail to comply with any legal obligation to which he is subject,
(c) that a miscarriage of justice has occurred, is occurring, or is likely to occur,
(d) that the health or safety of any individual has been, is being or is likely to be endangered,
(e) that the environment has been, is being, or is likely to be damaged, or
(f) that information tending to show any matter falling within any one of the preceding paragraphs has been, is being, or is likely to be deliberately concealed.

The employee must reasonably believe that one of the previously mentioned categories was satisfied. So, for example, in *Babula v Waltham Forest College*, an American lecturer believed that their predecessor had encouraged students in the class to celebrate the 9/11 attack on the Twin Towers. The lecturer disclosed this information to the College and was dismissed.[91] On appeal, the dismissal was found to have been unfair.

The allegation does not have to allege a contravention, still less identify the legislative provision contravened, but what is alleged must amount to a contravention.[92] The whistleblower must disclose facts of wrongdoing rather than general statements of law.[93]

To be a qualifying disclosure, the whistleblower must disclose the information in an acceptable manner, in other words, to the employer, or another

86 Section 104 Employment Rights Act 1996.
87 Regulation 7, The Part-time Workers (Prevention of Less Favourable Treatment) Regulations 2000; Regulation 17, The Agency Workers Regulations 2010.
88 Sections 45A and 101A Employment Rights Act 1996.
89 Sections 47B and 103A Employment Rights Act 1996.
90 Section 43B Employment Rights Act 1996.
91 *Babula v Waltham Forest College* [2004] IRLR 260, paras 82–3.
92 *Beneviste v Kingston University* [2006] EAT 0393/05, para 32.
93 *Cavendish Munro Professional Risks Management Ltd v Geduld* [2009] EAT 0195/09, paras 17, 26.

responsible person, a legal adviser, a Minister, or to a person prescribed by statute.[94]

The statute allows for disclosure to be made to the public where a worker reasonably believes the allegation is true, it is not made for personal gain, and it is reasonable to make the disclosure, and where various other requirements are satisfied, including that the worker believes they will be subject to a detriment if they raise the matter with the employer or where the worker reasonably believes the employer will conceal the information or where the worker has previously disclosed it to their employer.[95]

The statute also makes provision for disclosure after exceptionally serious failures.[96]

An ex-employee whistleblower can, in principle, bring a complaint regarding post-employment detriment arising from a protected disclosure made during the period of employment.[97] On the facts of the particular case, it is also open to ex-employees to bring claims resulting from post-employment disclosures.[98] However, where a whistleblower suffers a detriment outside employment, they cannot complain to the Tribunal.[99]

There is no counterpart to the reversal of the burden of proof in Equality Act claims. For an employee to succeed in a whistleblowing claim, they must show the fact that the protected disclosure "materially influenced (in the sense of being more than a trivial influence)" the employer's treatment of the whistleblower.[100]

94 Section 43C-F Employment Rights Act 1996.
95 Section 43G Employment Rights Act 1996.
96 Section 43H Employment Rights Act 1996.
97 *Woodward v Abbey National* [2006] EWCA Civ 822, para 68.
98 *Onyango v Berkeley* [2013] IRLR 338, para 8.
99 *Tiplady v City of Bradford* [2019] EWCA Civ 2180, para 45.
100 *NHS Manchester v Fecitt and Ors* [2011] EWCA Civ 1190, para 45.

3 Misconduct by the employee

The chapter addresses (i) allegations of misconduct against the employee, such as when they are accused of having used words which brought the employer into disrepute. The employer silences the employee by dismissing them from the workplace, leaving the Tribunal having to consider whether the dismissal was, in all the circumstances, fair. The chapter also considers a further theme of (ii) dismissals for some other substantial reason and their potential relevance to disputes relating to expression.

Conduct as a reason for dismissal

Conduct is one of six potentially fair reasons for dismissal.[1] In considering whether a conduct dismissal is fair, the Employment Tribunal is guided by the principles set out in *British Home Stores Ltd v Burchell*.[2] Under the *Burchell* test, the Tribunal must consider whether or not the employer had an honest belief in the guilt of the employee of misconduct at the time of dismissal. Second, the Tribunal considers whether the employer had, in their mind, reasonable grounds upon which to sustain that belief. Third, the Tribunal considers whether the employer, at the stage at which he formed the belief on those grounds, had carried out as much investigation into the matter as was reasonable in all the circumstances of the case.

In applying each of these tests, the Employment Tribunal allows a broad band of reasonable responses to the employer.[3] The band of reasonable responses test applies as much to the Respondent's investigation as it does to the decision to dismiss.[4]

If the answer to each of the three *British Home Stores v Burchell* questions is "yes", the ET must then decide on the reasonableness of the response by

1 Section 98, Employment Rights Act 1996.

2 *British Home Stores v Burchell* [1980] ICR 303, affirmed by the Court of Appeal in *Post Office v Foley* [2000] ICR 1283.

3 *Iceland Frozen Foods v Jones* [1982] ICR 17.

4 *Sainsbury's Supermarkets v Hitt* [2003] IRLR 23, para 30.

DOI: 10.4324/9781032724263-3

the employer. In performing the latter exercise, the ET must consider, by the objective standards of the hypothetical reasonable employer, rather than by reference to the ET's own subjective views, whether the employer has acted within a "band or range of reasonable responses" to the particular misconduct found of the particular employee.[5]

To justify dismissal, the misconduct must in some way reflect on the employer-employee relationship.[6] Examples of misconduct justifying dismissal include a refusal to obey a reasonable management instruction;[7] a breach of the employer's disciplinary standards;[8] and the commission of criminal offences or the concealing of offences committed in the past.[9]

Either a refusal to obey instruction or a breach of a company rule is not necessarily a fair reason for dismissal – it still falls to the employer, and ultimately the Tribunal, to decide whether the dismissal was a reasonable response to the breach.[10]

A negligent failure to carry out a task may justify summary dismissal; on the other hand, the negligence must be gross: "it ought not readily be found that a failure to act where there was no intentional decision to act contrary to or undermine the employer's policies constitutes such a grave act of misconduct as to justify summary dismissal".[11]

It is unreasonable to dismiss an employee for failure to comply with a material term of an employment contract of which the employee was unaware and of which they could not reasonably have been aware.[12]

If an employer has admitted misconduct, for example, in separate criminal proceedings, the employer can reasonably act on that assumption that the misconduct took place.[13] However, if the employee disputes intending to commit an act of misconduct, asserts that their error was honest, or has points to make in mitigation, the employer must consider them.[14] In any case, the employer must still follow a fair procedure.[15] It is particularly important that employers take seriously their responsibilities to conduct a fair investigation where, as on the facts of that case, the employee's reputation or ability to work in their chosen field of employment is potentially at risk.[16]

5 *Graham v The Secretary of State for Work and Pensions* [2012] EWCA Civ 903, para 36.
6 *Thomson v Alloa Motor Co Ltd* [1983] IRLR 403.
7 *Famborough v Governors of Edinburgh College of Art* [1974] IRLR 245.
8 *McPhie and McDermott v Wimpey Waste Management Ltd* [1981] IRLR 316.
9 *Nottinghamshire County Council v Bowly* [1978] IRLR 252; *Moore v C and A Modes* [1981] IRLR 71; *Norfolk County Council v Barnard* [1979] IRLR 220.
10 *Ladbroke Racing Limited v Arnott* [1983] IRLR 154.
11 *Adesokan v Sainsbury's* [2017] EWCA Civ 22, para 24.
12 *Donachie v Allied Suppliers Limited* EAT 46/80.
13 *RSPB v Croucher* [1984] IRLR 425.
14 *John Lewis plc v Coyne* [2001] IRLR 139.
15 *Whitbread plc v Hall* [2001] IRLR 275.
16 *Salford Royal NHS Foundation Trust v Roldan* [2010] EWCA Civ 522, para 13.

In investigating a conduct dismissal, the employer must follow the relevant ACAS Code. An unreasonable failure to do so may result in the employer increasing the damages award to the employee by up to 25%.[17] The ACAS Code of Practice on disciplinary and grievance procedures provides, amongst other things, that where an employee is accused of a first act of misconduct, the normal choice open to the employer will be between disregarding the warning and punishing, up to a normal maximum of a final written warning. That punishment will be appropriate where the employee's actions have had, or are liable to have, a serious or harmful impact on the organisation.[18]

The Code goes on to provide that some acts, termed gross misconduct, are so serious in themselves or have such serious consequences that they may call for dismissal without notice for a first offence. But, a fair disciplinary process should always be followed before dismissing for gross misconduct.[19]

Gross misconduct

Gross misconduct is conduct which makes it impossible for an employer to retain an employee in employment. This is an objective test:

> Of course there may be misconduct in a servant which will not justify the determination of the contract of service by one of the parties to it against the will of the other. On the other hand misconduct inconsistent with the fulfilment of the express or implied conditions of service will justify dismissal.[20]

If summary dismissal is claimed to be justifiable, the question must be whether the conduct complained of is such as to show the servant to have disregarded the essential conditions of the contract of service.[21]

For a single act of misconduct to justify dismissal, it must be serious, willful, and obvious. The misconduct must be such that the employee would plainly recognise it as conduct which would merit summary dismissal if discovered by his employers.[22]

Where the Tribunal accepts that gross misconduct is made out, it must nevertheless go on to make a separate analysis of whether that misconduct justified dismissal since it is at least conceptually possible that an employee was guilty of gross misconduct and that a dismissal for it would nonetheless

17 Section 207A of the Trade Union and Labour Relations (Consolidation) Act 1992.
18 ACAS Code, para 20.
19 ACAS Code, para 23.
20 *Neary v Dean of Westminster* [1999] IRLR 288, para 22.
21 *Laws v London Chronicle Ltd* (1959) 2 All ER 285.
22 *Bishop v Graham Group plc* [1999] EAT 800/98.

be unfair (e.g., because of honesty on the part of the employee or contrition or long good service, etc.).[23]

Reputational harm

In many freedom of expression cases, at the core of the employer's case against the employee is the complaint that the behaviour of the latter has caused damage to the business's reputation and the willingness of other organisations to trade with it. While many first-instance cases turn on whether any reputational harm was, in fact, caused, there can be no dispute that, in principle, such damage is capable of justifying dismissal.

In *Post Office v Liddiard*, the Court of Appeal considered a Post Office employee who had been convicted of assaulting a French police officer during the 1998 World Cup. He was subsequently identified by a national newspaper and dismissed for bringing the Post Office into disrepute. The Tribunal found that Liddiard had an excellent employment record, and the misconduct was unrelated to his employment. It held that the decision to dismiss had been unfairly influenced by press coverage. The Court of Appeal subsequently remitted the matter back to a different Tribunal for a fresh hearing.[24]

One reason for the Court of Appeal's difficulty in understanding the Tribunal's decision was that, although Mr Liddiard asserted his innocence of the assault and the Tribunal accepted his account, he had been convicted. Where a person has been convicted of a crime, the Tribunal will ordinarily treat the conviction as determinative.[25]

Misconduct taking the form of expression: refusal to obey an order

Where an employee refuses to act on an instruction given by their employer, art 10 principles may be engaged if, for example, the opinions of the employee required them to express opinions and to keep on doing so, even where instructed by the employer to desist. In those circumstances, the employer will seek to persuade the Tribunal that the reason for dismissal was misconduct, i.e., refusing to obey a reasonable order. While the employee is likely to argue that the real reason for dismissal was the employer's unreasonable restriction of their entitlement to freedom of expression.

There have been some cases where an employer orders an employee to communicate in a certain way, and the employee refuses. The 1981 Court of Appeal case of *Union of Construction Allied Trades and Technicians v*

23 *Brito-Babapulle v Ealing Hospital NHS Trust* [2014] EWCA Civ 1626, paras 10–11.
24 *Post Office v Liddiard* [2001] EWCA Civ 940, paras 14, 21.
25 *P v Nottinghamshire County Council* [1992] IRLR 362.

Brain,[26] a publication officer was responsible for the production of a trade union journal, *UCATT Viewpoint*, under the direction of the union's General Secretary. The journal published an article which was highly critical of the employers' magazine, *Construction News*. A libel action was brought against the publication officer, though he had no responsibility for the original article. The libel claim was settled. As part of the terms of the settlement, the employee was required to sign a statement saying that neither he nor any union officers would repeat the libel. The employee had not been consulted about the settlement which was approved by the union's executive. After taking legal advice from a solicitor provided by his own trade union, he refused to sign the agreement even though UCATT insisted that he should. The Court of Appeal confirmed the original Tribunal's finding that the dismissal was unfair. Lord Justice Lawton held that where the dismissal is for a refusal to obey an instruction the primary factor to be considered is whether the employee was or could have been acting reasonably in disobeying the instruction.

Since the *UCATT* case, there have been a number of article 10 decisions which similarly protect people from having to express themselves in a way in which they do not want to be compelled to, including *Buscarini v San Marino*,[27] concerning members of the San Marino Parliament who were required to swear a Christian oath; *Lee v Ashers*, concerning bakers who would not be compelled to make a cake supporting the right of LGBT people to marry,[28] and *Royal Bahamas Defence Force v Laramore*, where a petty officer who had converted from Christianity to Islam was ordered to remove his cap during prayers.[29]

Breaches of discipline

Another main form of misconduct is where an employee breaches the employer's disciplinary code. An example, albeit one predating the Human Rights Act 1998 or the 2003 Regulations outlawing discrimination on the grounds of religion or belief, was the 1975 case of *Singh v Lyons Maid Ltd.* Mr Singh, who worked in an ice cream factory, was absent over Christmas 1975, and when he returned to work, he had grown a beard. He refused to shave it off and stated that he intended to wear it for religious reasons. The company dismissed Mr Singh. He argued that the rule against wearing beards was unjustified. The Tribunal held the dismissal to be fair and observed, "We can see nothing unreasonable in a dismissal which is based on a refusal by the employee to comply with a term of his contract".[30] Were the same facts to come to a Tribunal today,

26 *Union of Construction Allied Trades and Technicians v Brain* [1981] IRLR 224.

27 *Buscarini v San Marino* (1999) 30 EHRR 208.

28 *Lee v Ashers Baking Company* [2018] UKSC 49, para 55.

29 *Royal Bahamas Defence Force v Laramore* (2017) 1 WLR 2752, para 29.

30 *Singh v Lyons Maid Ltd* [1975] IRLR 328.

Mr Singh might challenge the dismissal as indirect discrimination under the Equality Act. So, in the 2018 case of *Sethi v Elements Personnel Services Ltd*, a "no beards" rule was found to discriminate against Sikhs indirectly.[31]

Criminal offences

A number of historic cases concerned criminal behaviour which is no longer considered unlawful, in particular, sexual acts by gay men. The 1980 case of *Saunders v Scottish National Camps Association* concerned a handyman at a camp for children and teenagers, who was dismissed because it was discovered that he had had sex with men, although he had not received any conviction. The employer dismissed him, relying on part on the stereotypical assumption that gay men were perceived to be likely to seek sexual encounters with children. Saunders said he was not interested in young persons and could keep his private life separate from his work. The Appeal Tribunal upheld his dismissal.[32]

> In 2003, the Employment Appeal Tribunal held that the employer's reliance on acts done in a person's private life as a plausible justification for dismissal would mean that cases involving similar facts would need to be considered differently.[33]

Misconduct online

Several reported misconduct dismissals have concerned language used online. Part of the conceptual difficulty caused by such cases is the long-standing cultural assumption, to some extent reflected in our law, that spoken words are transient and incapable of doing lasting harm, while written words have greater weight. This distinction is reflected in the differences between the law of libel and of slander. As long ago as the seventeenth century, the Chief Justice of the King's Bench, Matthew Hale, held that the written form "contains more malice than if [the words] had once been spoken".[34] From the perspective of misconduct, words used online sit at an awkward point between written and spoken language. Like the latter, they can be expressed quickly and to their maker's regret. Like the former, they have the capacity to hang around, be shared by large numbers of people, and receive a wide audience.

31 *Sethi v Elements Personnel Services Ltd* [2018] ET case no 2300234/2018.

32 *Saunders v Scottish National Camps* [1980] IRLR 174; similar reasoning could also be seen in *Wiseman v Salford City Council* [1981] IRLR 202.

33 *X v Y* [2003] EAT 0765/02, paras 33–4.

34 *King v Lake* [1668] Hard 470.

Online words and reputational harm

In a case heard in the High Court, *Smith v Trafford Housing*,[35] Mr Justice Briggs considered how the employer should have responded when an employee had publicly expressed his opposition to gay marriage, in that way potentially jeopardising the employer's relationship with its customers. Under Mr Smith's employment contract, the Trust could demote him as a disciplinary sanction for misconduct, which included a breach of company rules or failure to reach the required standards in regard to conduct. It stated that conduct that occurred outside working hours or away from the premises of the Trust might have been considered a breach of discipline and been subject to disciplinary procedures. The Trust's Code of Conduct provided that

> employees are required to act in a non-confrontational, non-judgmental manner with all customers, with their family/friends and colleagues. The Trust is a non-political, non-denominational organisation and employees should not attempt to promote their political or religious views. . . . Customers, their friends and family and colleagues must always be treated with dignity and respect.[36]

The Trust's Equal Opportunities Policy provided that

> employees have a responsibility to treat their colleagues, tenants, third party suppliers and members of the public with dignity and respect being non-judgmental in approach and not engaging in any conduct which may make another person feel uncomfortable, embarrassed or upset.[37]

Mr Smith was a practising Christian. He also posted on Facebook occasionally. At the time of his posts, he had 201 Facebook friends, most of them fellow Christians. Some 45 of them were fellow employees of the Trust.

Briggs J found that Mr Smith's postings about gay marriage could not have brought the Trust into disrepute.[38] In light of his occasional posting and modest audience, as well as the positions taken by the Trust, no reasonable reader of Mr Smith's Facebook wall page could have concluded that his posts were made on the Trust's behalf.

35 *Smith v Trafford Housing Trust* [2013] IRLR 86.
36 *Smith v Trafford*, para 22.
37 *Smith v Trafford*, para 24.
38 *Smith v Trafford*, paras 62–4.

One of the Trust's obligations was to promote equality and, therefore, diversity of opinion among its staff. Inevitably, that meant recruiting people holding different opinions:

> Again, I cannot envisage how any such loss of reputation would arise in the mind of any reasonable reader of Mr Smith's postings, whether in the Albert Kennedy organisation or otherwise. The Trust prides itself on encouraging diversity both among its customers and its employees, and that encouragement of diversity forms part of its no doubt well-deserved reputation. But the encouragement of diversity in the recruitment of employees inevitably involves employing persons with widely different religious and political beliefs and views, some of which, however moderately expressed, may cause distress among the holders of deeply felt opposite views.[39]

Smith v Trafford in the employment courts

Smith v Trafford Housing Trust was cited with approval by the Employment Appeal Tribunal in *Game Retail Ltd v Laws*. In that case, over a year altogether, a store manager posted numerous derogatory messages about the business's customers on Twitter. His account was followed by more than 60 other stories in the business. The matter was investigated, and the manager was dismissed. The EAT held:

> There is a balance to be drawn between an employer's desire to remove or reduce reputational risk from social media communications by its employees and the employee's right of freedom of expression; see *Smith*. . . Generally speaking, employees must have the right to express themselves, providing it does not infringe on their employment and/or is outside the work context.[40]

The reliance on *Smith v Trafford Housing Trust* (i.e., a civil case) in the Employment Tribunal was approved in *London Borough of Hammersmith and Fulham v Keable*.[41] Mr Keable was a Public Protection and Safety Officer at the London Borough of Hammersmith and Fulham. In the spring of 2018, a rally was held outside Parliament to criticise the then-leader of the Labour Party, Jeremy Corbyn, who was accused of antisemitism. Keable had been outside Parliament, not with the main protest, but with a smaller counter-protest called by a pro-Corbyn campaign, Jewish Voice for Labour. As the participants from the two events mingled, Keable and one of the Enough is Enough

39 *Smith v Trafford*, para 62.

40 *Game Retail Ltd v Laws* [2014] EAT 0188/14, para 46.

41 *London Borough of Hammersmith and Fulham v Keable* [2022] IRLR 4.

demonstrators found themselves talking while a BBC journalist, David Grossman, filmed their conversation on his mobile phone. The anti-Corbyn demonstrator pointed out the antisemitic character of the Mear One mural. Keable replied that Corbyn had a life-long history of anti-racism. Keable told the anti-Corbyn demonstrator: "the Nazis were antisemitic . . . the Zionist movement at the time collaborated with them".[42]

Without asking Keable's permission, the BBC journalist placed the film on his Twitter feed, where it received numerous comments. The Conservative MP for Hammersmith and Fulham, Greg Hands, shared the post. Soon after, Keable was dismissed. When asked about the conversation, Keable apologised for any offence he had caused. He was a long-standing employee, and the employer gave no real consideration to a sanction short of dismissal. Although the words were inappropriate, the employer did not suggest that they were antisemitic. The conversation between Keable and the demonstrator had been quiet and respectful. Moreover, he was at the event in his private time, in his own clothes.[43]

The Tribunal found his dismissal contrary to Mr Keable's article 10 right to freedom of expression. An employee's "legitimate exercise of his right to freedom of expression, which was not suggested to be unlawful, away from the workplace and with no link to the workplace at the time", could not amount to misconduct justifying his dismissal.[44] On Appeal, the EAT upheld both the Tribunal's reasoning and its findings, including an order reinstating Mr Keable to his employment with the Respondent.

First-instance social media cases include *Blue v Food Standards Agency*, in which an employee was found to have been unfairly dismissed after liking a comment referring to an attack on his manager.[45] In *Weeks v Everything Everywhere*, an employee was fairly dismissed for repeatedly referring to his workplace as "Dante's Inferno", and refused to withdraw those comments when asked.[46] Seemingly very similar conduct received a different treatment in *Trasler v B&Q*, however, where an employee who posted, "This place of work is beyond a fucking joke", and the dismissal was found to be unfair.[47] In *Webb v London Underground*, a London underground manager was dismissed for sharing on Facebook a post which referred to a black victim of a killing shooting by asking, "The media and the left made George Floyd into a Martyr. But who was he really?", before listing a series of allegations which tended to denigrate him. The Tribunal criticised the dismissing officer for taking an over-narrow approach in which no options were considered other than an apology or dismissal, and the dismissal was found to be unfair.[48]

42 *Keable v Hammersmith and Fulham*, para 31.
43 *Keable v Hammersmith and Fulham*, para 177.
44 *Keable v Hammersmith and Fulham*, para 130.
45 *Blue v Food Standards Agency* [2015] ETS case no 4100341/2014.
46 *Weeks v Everything Everywhere Ltd* [2013] ET case no 2503016/2012.
47 *Trasler v B&Q* [2013] ET case no 1200504/2012.
48 *Webb v London Underground* [2023] WL 02286998.

Polkey and contributory fault

Even in a case where the employee succeeds in obtaining a finding that a misconduct dismissal was unfair, it remains open to the employer to argue that the employee was blameworthy and contributed to his dismissal and/or that had it followed a fair conduct investigation, the employer would have dismissed anyway.

By section 122(2) Employment Rights Act 1996 ("ERA"), where the Tribunal considers that any conduct of the complainant before the dismissal was such that it would be just and equitable to reduce the amount of the basic award, the Tribunal shall make such a reduction. By s123(6) ERA, where the Tribunal finds that the dismissal was to any extent caused or contributed to by any action of the complainant, it shall reduce the amount of the compensatory award by such proportion as it considers just and equitable.[49]

In *Nelson v BBC (No 2)*,[50] the Court of Appeal said that three factors must be satisfied if the Tribunal is to find contributory conduct: first, the action must be culpable and blameworthy. Second, it must actually have caused or contributed to the dismissal. Third, it must be just and equitable to reduce the award by the proportion specified.

As an example of contributory fault, in *Brown v Castlerock Group Ltd*, an employee was dismissed for gross misconduct in stealing money from one of the firm's clients. She brought proceedings for unfair dismissal. The Tribunal held that the employer had shown on the balance of probabilities that she had committed the theft. However, there had been serious lapses in the procedure adopted by the firm when conducting its inquiries, and so the dismissal was unfair on that ground. The Tribunal reduced the employee's contribution to zero to reflect their contributory fault.[51]

By contrast, in *Croydon Health Services NHS Trust v Brown*,[52] HHJ Peter Clark considered an NHS contractor with a senior role who had authorised a payment to his brother without completing the documents required of him. The Employment Appeal Tribunal reduced the employee's award by just 25 percent.

The notion that the employer would have dismissed in any event arises from the nature of the employee's claim for compensation; they want compensation for the period after their dismissal. Issues for the Tribunal may include the health of a Claimant and whether that would have permitted the employment to continue; whether the Claimant might retire and, if so, when; whether the Claimant might, for her own purposes, wish to leave the job. The employer may raise any number of factual considerations, such as the likelihood that they were going to

49 *Optikinetics Limited v Whooley* [1999] ICR 984.

50 *Nelson v BBC (No 2)* [1980] ICR 110.

51 *Brown v Castlerock Group Ltd* [2022] EAT 5.

52 *Croydon Health Services NHS Trust v Brown* [2013] EAT 0601/11.

reduce staff numbers or close the workplace, etc. The Tribunal has to consider not a hypothetical fair employer but has to assess the actions of the employer who is before the Tribunal, on the assumption that the employer would this time have acted fairly,[53] though it did not do so beforehand. Deductions of this sort are commonly referred to as "*Polkey*" deductions in acknowledgment of the case where they were first considered.[54]

Some other substantial reasons: threat to reputation

As noted previously, in a number of misconduct cases, the employer has argued that dismissal was inevitable on the ground of the threat to its reputation. In cases where an employer has been convicted of criminal conduct – i.e., the fact of misconduct is undeniable – these cases can and should be analysed under the heading of conduct. There are also, however, cases where the fact or otherwise of misconduct or unclear, but the reality of reputational threat is, from the employer's perspective, undeniable. That might happen, for example, if serious criminal allegations are made, there is no likelihood of their determination on any timescale which can assist the employer. These cases, while conceptually close to misconduct dismissals, are ultimately distinct from them.

While, in misconduct cases, the question of whether a dismissal is capable of being fair is not ordinarily asked, in cases where the employer relies on some other substantial reason, the question must be asked, "In order to justify dismissal the breakdown in trust must be a substantial reason. Tribunals and courts must not dilute that requirement".[55]

The different structure of analysis in some other substantial reason dismissals arises because this category is broader than misconduct and encompasses a number of "no-fault" dismissals, e.g., mutual terminations and ineffective resignations. In neither of those situations would it normally be appropriate for a Tribunal to determine fairness by focusing principally on the adequacy of the employer's investigation?

A number of other substantial reasons dismissals have arisen as a result of errors on the part of the employer. In those cases, the key question is whether it is reasonable for the employee to bear the consequences of the employer's error.[56]

A good illustration of the potential complexities of these dismissals is *Leach v the Office of Communications.* There, the employer received information from the police concerning serious but untested allegations of child

53 *Johnson v Roller World* [2010] EAT 0237/10.

54 *Polkey v AE Dayton Services Ltd* [1988] ICR 142. The same principles apply to Equality Act claims: *Abbey National plc v Chagger* [2010] ICR 398.

55 *Leach v the Office of Communications* [2012] ICR 1269 at 1272A.

56 *Eversheds v De Belin* [2011] ICR 1137, 1151C-D; also *Docherty v SW Global Resourcing Ltd* 2014 SC 180, para 20.

sex abuse by the Claimant overseas. The Respondent did not seek to justify dismissal on the basis that the Claimant was, in fact, guilty of the matters disclosed to it. Rather, it argued that the mere making of an allegation that the Claimant was a threat to children meant that the fundamental relationship of trust and confidence between the parties had broken down.

While the Employment Appeal Tribunal upheld the judgment of the Tribunal, however, it set out its concerns with the reliance on some other substantial reason rather than conduct and the conceptual difficulties which follows from that choice:

> It sticks in the throat that an employee may lose his job, or perhaps in practice any chance of obtaining further employment, on the basis of allegations which he has had no opportunity to challenge in any court of law-or may indeed have successfully challenged.[57]

This warning against the overuse of some other substantial reason chimes with warnings given in a number of other appeals to the higher courts.[58]

There have been, in addition, a few cases where some other substantial reason was used as a justification for dismissal. Many of these might just as well be characterised as disputes of opinion or attempt to limit free expression, although that is not necessarily how the cases were analysed when they came before the Tribunal. So, for example, in the 1975 case of *Treganowan v Robert Knee*, a woman in an office caused dissent among her colleagues. She had an illegitimate child and had begun dating a man who was much younger than she was. The employer characterised the Claimant's expression of her views as causing "a difference of opinion as to the merits of the permissive society". A Tribunal held that this constituted "some other substantial reason" and the dismissal was fair, a decision upheld on appeal. It is hard to see how an attempted dismissal of similar facts today could survive the much more robust protection of freedom of opinion that now exists under article 10.[59]

57 *Leach*, para 37.

58 *Governing Body of Tubbenden Primary School v Sylvester* EAT 0527/11; *McFarlane v Relate Avon Ltd* [2010] ICR 507, para 40.

59 *Treganowan v Robert Knee and Co Ltd* [1975] IRLR 247.

4 Breaches by the employer

This chapter considers various ways in which employers limit the expression of their employees and which are capable of being unlawful: (i) the law in general in relation to breaches of the employment contract and examples of breaches in relation to expression, (ii) blacklisting, (iii) surveillance, (iv) "retro-dismissal" (i.e., the trawling of data in order to justify disciplinary action against an employee which is motivated by the desire to punish the employee for another reason), and (v) employment pre-screening, in particular where that overlaps with the unjustifiable sentiment, including anti-union sentiment. The chapter sets out the extent to which these processes are presently lawful, as well as some of the key weaknesses in the law's current protection of employees. It concludes with a discussion of (vi) non-disclosure agreements, and in particular, their use by employers to conceal allegations of misconduct

Breaches of the employment contract: fundamental breaches

As explained in Chapter 2, there is no rule that an employer must act reasonably in the workplace. The nearest we have such a rule is the power, open to the employee, to resign in response to a repudiatory breach of contract, after which the employee is entitled to treat the employment contract as being at an end.

The 1978 case of *Western Excavating v Sharp* sets out four conditions which required to be met for the employee to claim constructive dismissal: (i) There must be a breach of contract by the employer. This may be either an actual breach or an anticipatory breach. (ii) That breach must be sufficiently important to justify the employee resigning, or else it must be the last in a series of incidents which justify his leaving. (iii) The employee must leave in response to the breach and not for some other, unconnected reason. (iv) The employee must not delay too long in terminating the contract in response to

DOI: 10.4324/9781032724263-4

the employer's breach; otherwise, they may be deemed to have waived the breach and agreed to vary the contract[1]

When an employee resigns, they must establish not merely that they were constructively dismissed but also that it was unfair according to section 98 test of reasonableness. At this stage only, the employee needs to show that dismissal was outside the range of reasonable responses.[2]

At its most essential, the employment contract is an agreement between two parties in which one agrees to work and the other agrees to provide remuneration. For that reason, when the courts have set out behaviour which will always amount to a repudiatory breach, they have set out matters which reflect this wage-work relationship, as when an employer unilaterally reduces the pay of the employee;[3] unilaterally changes the employee's duties;[4] insists upon the employee extending their working hours to perform duties which they are not contractually required to do;[5] or fails to provide the employee with the work that he or she is employed to do.[6] Breaches of an employee's right to freedom of expression are capable of being breaches of a fundamental term, but whether they actually cross this threshold will depend on the facts.

Relevant terms

The term most commonly relied on by the employee is the employer's obligation of trust and confidence; the employer shall not, without reasonable and proper cause conduct itself in a manner calculated and likely to destroy or seriously damage the relationship of confidence and trust between employer and employee.[7] In assessing whether conduct is of that seriousness, the test is an objective one, asking whether an employee could be expected to put up with the conduct, not the subjective intention of the employer.[8]

Other employer breaches which have been treated as fundamental include refusing to investigate complaints promptly and reasonably;[9] permitting an employee to suffer unacceptable abuse;[10] and singling an employee out for unfavourable treatment.[11]

1 *Western Excavating v Sharp* [1978] IRLR 27.
2 *Buckland v Bournemouth University Higher Education Corp* [2010] EWCA Civ 121.
3 *Industrial Rubber Products v Gillon* [1977] IRLR 389.
4 *Coleman v S and W Baldwin* [1977] IRLR 342; *Genower v Ealing Hammersmith and Hounslow Area Health Authority* [1980] IRLR 297; *Pedersen v Camden London Borough Council* [1981] IRLR 173; *Land Securities Trillium Ltd v Thornley* [2005] IRLR 765.
5 *Derby City Council v Marshall* [1979] IRLR 261.
6 *Lees v Imperial College of Science, Technology and Medicine* EAT 0288/15.
7 *Malik v Bank of Credit and Commerce International SA* [1997] IRLR 462.
8 *Leeds Dental Ltd v Rose* [2014] ICR 94.
9 *British Aircraft Corp v Austin* [1978] IRLR 332.
10 *Palmanor Ltd v Cedron* [1978] IRLR 303.
11 *FC Gardner Ltd v Beresford* [1978] IRLR 63.

One way in which freedom of expression cases come to the Tribunal is as claims for breach of the Equality Act. There is no authority to the effect that any breach of that Act will always be a breach of a fundamental term. On the other hand, there are a number of cases where infringements of that Act have been interpreted as if they were fundamental breaches. For example, in *Bracebridge v Darby*, a failure to investigate a grievance brought under the Act had been a fundamental breach permitting the employee to resign.[12]

In *Nottinghamshire County Council v Meikle*, a claim brought by a teacher with a degenerative visual impairment, a local authority was found to have failed to make reasonable adjustments to written materials and to a teaching schedule and location of duties. The Tribunal did not accept that the breach was fundamental. The Court of Appeal reversed that decision.[13]

Breaches falling short of a fundamental breach

In cases where the employee is faced with a breach of article 10, which falls short of a fundamental breach of the employment contract, or where the employee does not wish to enforce a breach through bringing a claim for unfair constructive dismissal (a procedure which is costly, and risky), they do have certain other options.

The employee may be able to bring an Equality Act claim to the Tribunal, potentially as a claim for detriment in reliance on the protected characteristic of religion or belief or another characteristic if relevant. It is entirely normal for such claims to be brought by an employee who remains in employment.

In the right case, an employee[14] might seek to enforce a right under article 10 by bringing proceedings probably in the High Court for damages for a breach of that right. One of the potential advantages of that process is that the High Court, unlike the Tribunal, has the power to grant injunctions. Therefore, it is open in principle to the employee not merely to seek damages but also an order prohibiting any limit on their freedom of expression. In practice, these applications are rare because, in civil proceedings, costs follow the event, in contrast to employment law, where costs are only ordered after unreasonable conduct.[15] The other significant risk associated is that in High

12 *Bracebridge Engineering Ltd v Darby* [1990] IRLR 3.

13 *Nottinghamshire County Council v Meikle* [2004] EWCA Civ 859, paras 33–9.

14 Proceedings in the civil courts can also be used to obtain a declaration that the dismissal of a former employee office-holder was unlawful. Proceeding in civil litigation rather than the Employment Tribunal should be permitted when the Tribunal does not supply an "equally convenient and effective" remedy. *Shoesmith, R (on the application of) v OFSTED and Ors* [2011] EWCA Civ 642, para 99.

15 Rules 74–7, the Employment Tribunals Rules of Procedure, 2013.

Court proceedings, unlike most[16] Tribunal proceedings, the employer may counterclaim.

Blacklisting

The practice of compiling data on employees and potential employees without their consent in order to sanction them is, in principle, unlawful. Amongst other things, it is a criminal offence under section 55(1) of the Data Protection Act 1998:

> A person must not knowingly or recklessly, without the consent of the data controller –
>
> (a) obtain or disclose personal data or the information contained in personal data, or
> (b) procure the disclosure to another person of the information contained in personal data.

There are various statutory defences under the Act: the necessity to prevent or detect crime, authorisation under an enactment, public interest, etc.

In addition, the Employment Relations Act 1999 (Blacklists) Regulations 2010 create a tort enforceable in the Employment Tribunal where an employer refuses to employ (reg 5) or an employment agency refuses its services to a person for a reason related to a prohibited list, and the agency or employer has "compile[d], use[d], s[old] or suppl[ied] a prohibited list". A prohibited list is one that:

> (a) contains details of persons who are or have been members of trade unions or persons who are taking part or have taken part in the activities of trade unions, and (b) is compiled with a view to being used by employers or employment agencies for the purposes of discrimination in relation to recruitment or in relation to the treatment of workers [reg 3].[17]

The blacklisting regulations also prohibit employers from causing an employee a detriment short of dismissal for a reason relating to a prohibited list (reg 9).

16 Article 3 of the Employment Tribunals Extension of Jurisdiction (England and Wales) Order 1994 permits employees to bring claims for damages (although not for personal injury) where the claim arises or is outstanding on the termination of the employee's employment. There are few reported cases of the operation of counterclaims in the Tribunal. In *Cortel v Shah* [2019] EAT 0252/18, it was found that such counterclaims could continue where the original claim was withdrawn.

17 The list need not be in writing: *Miller v Interserve Industrial Services Ltd* [2012] EAT 0244/12, para 7.

In deciding whether a person has been blacklisted, the Tribunal will apply the same test as in discrimination law, namely, what was the reason why the employer took the decision that it did.[18] The Claimants only needed to show that their trade union membership or activities were a significant part of the employer's mental processes; they do not need to have been the principal reason. "But for" causation link is not enough: the Claimants' trade union membership or activities must have been at least part of what operated consciously or subconsciously on the employer's mind to make its managers do what they did.[19]

Blacklisting: key cases

The practice of blacklisting has been a matter of public discussion since 2009 when the Information Commissioner's Office raided the headquarters of an organisation known as the Consulting Association. This business had an annual turnover in excess of £100,000 and held information on workers' names, dates of birth, addresses, national insurance numbers, employment history, and union or political affiliations. A total of 44 construction companies subscribed to the Association, and it held various lists, including one of 3,213 construction workers and environmental activists.

The first legal process to arise from the raid was a criminal prosecution of the Consulting Association's Chief Officer, Mr Ian Kerr, brought by the ICO for multiple breaches of section 55 of the DPA. The ICO had been tipped off that there was a construction industry blacklist and seized it. The ICO did not attempt to seize any other data held by Mr Kerr. He then destroyed his other data. Only Mr Kerr was prosecuted, not the companies which supplied and used the data. He was fined a mere £5,000.

After 2009, 50 blacklisted construction workers brought claims to the Employment Tribunal. These were not claims for blacklisting (the regulations had not yet been made) or breach of data protection rules (which are not directly enforceable in the Tribunal) but for employment law torts (unfair dismissal or a failure to appoint a job applicant). A key obstacle for the workers was the time limit in the Employment Tribunals, under which claims may only be brought within three months unless it was not reasonably practicable to do so, and time may be extended but only for a limited further time, as long as is reasonable. All but two claims ultimately failed this hurdle and were struck out.[20]

18 *Nagarajan v London Regional Transport* [1999] ICR 877, at pp 884–6.

19 *Miller and Ors v Interserve Industrial Services Ltd* [2013] ICR 445, paras 14, 19–20.

20 Four of the cases were appealed: *Cullinane v Balfour Beatty Engineering Services Ltd* [2010] EAT 0537/10, *Tattersfield v Balfour Beatty Engineering Services Ltd* [2011] 3 WLUK 58 and *Balfour Beatty Engineering Services v Allen* [2011] EAT 0236/11; *Nolan v Balfour Beatty Engineering Services* [2011] EAT 0109/11.

The only claim following the blacklisting raids to have reached the higher courts was *Smith v Carillion (JM) Ltd.*[21] A Tribunal held that Mr Smith's claim had been brought in time. Carillion admitted blacklisting but argued that there had been no contract between it and Mr Smith, who was an agency worker, and that it was not liable for its breaches since, in ordinary employment law, no one other than an employee may sue for detriment short of dismissal. But, in blacklisting Mr Smith, Carillion had infringed his rights under article 8 ECHR, which protects home and private life.

The key issue on appeal to the Court of Appeal was that Mr Smith was an agency worker. He invited the Court to read and give effect to section 146 of the Trade Union and Labour Relations (Consolidation) Act 1992, which protects workers from detriment on grounds of trade union membership, as if, at the time Mr Smith was blacklisted, it had extended the protection to agency workers who were not employees of their end-user (but who had, as in the case of Mr Smith, been blacklisted by them). However, rather than using Mr Smith's case to read the statute purposively to extend protection, the Court of Appeal chose to reinforce the judge-made exclusion of agency workers from the ordinary protection of employment law. Given the prevalence of agency workers in construction and given the role of the construction industry as the one in which blacklisting has been best documented, this was a significant restriction on the effectiveness of the regulations in protecting workers.

A number of employment claims have been heard relating to post-2009 blacklisting, including *Morris v Electrical Installation Services Limited*, which was heard at the Employment Tribunal in 2013.[22] In that case, an electrician working on a major rail construction project was identified by the project's managers as a trade unionist, and pressure was put on the sub-contractor to dismiss him.[23]

There were three preliminary hearings in *Morris*. The worker maintained that he had sufficient evidence of blacklisting so that the contractors should be obliged to disclose all email exchanges taking place between a small group of their managers, who had been associated previously with the Consulting Association. The employer refused to disclose any information, saying that the costs of checking its email addresses would be disproportionate and that the Claimant's case could not succeed. The case was later settled.

Eventually, in May 2016, group litigation in the High Court by the blacklisted workers resulted in a public apology and the payment of significant compensation. In that case ("The Construction Industry Vetting Information Group Litigation"), the claimants argued that, where an employer liaises with

21 *Smith v Carillion (JM) Ltd* [2015] IRLR 467.

22 *Morris v Electrical Installation Services Limited and Others* [2013] ET case no 2205900/2012.

23 The facts of the case were simultaneously discussed in House of Commons Scottish Affairs Select Committee, *Blacklisting in Employment* (London: House of Commons, 2013), p Q2634.

a third-party blacklisting company, in so doing, they commit a tort which is actionable in the civil courts as a claim for damages arising from a breach of the Data Protection Act or articles 8, 11 or 14 of the European Convention on Human Rights or as a conspiracy to breach a contract. The settled nature of the litigation means that those concepts have never been publicly tested.

Surveillance

In 1997, a senior police officer, Ms Halford, sued the United Kingdom for failing to protect her private life and correspondence, pursuant to article 8 ECHR. Ms Halford had instituted a sex discrimination claim against her employer, causing the force to intercept her calls. Her complaint succeeded. Part of the reason it succeeded was that the calls were made on a private telephone network, and there was at that time no legal restriction on surveillance of such networks; therefore, there was no opportunity for the state to say that the employer's acts were in accordance with the law.

In 2007, a second article 8 claimant also succeeded at the ECtHR.[24] Ms Copland was a college administrator suspected by her former lover (the College's Deputy Principal) of having a relationship with a colleague. The College monitored telephone, email, and internet. Her step-daughter was contacted by the College and asked about the emails.

In 2009, a further article 8 claim was unsuccessful, involving a claimant, Mr Pay. Strictly, the claim was not about monitoring, as such, but rather the extent to which an employer can rely on private data in dismissing. However, the case went a considerable way towards saying that employers could hold and rely on such data.[25] The case concerned a probation officer who, on his weekends, took part in BDSM activities.[26] He had disclosed his membership in an organisation which carried out sexual activities but not its character to his employer. On the organisation's website, there were photographs of him, albeit his face was obscured to make it harder to identify him personally. The service received an anonymous fax tipping it off about his activities and dismissed him. The Court of Appeal found that there was no breach of article 8.

Strasbourg determined the case slightly differently, finding that there had arguably been a breach of article 8 and the right to privacy. Mr Pay had attended nightclubs which were likely to be frequented only by a select group of like-minded people, and the images of him were anonymised. Assuming that the right to privacy was engaged, however, as a probation officer working

24 *Copland v UK* [2007] ECHR 253.

25 *Pay v United Kingdom 32792/05* [2009] IRLR 139.

26 One way to make sense of the decision may be to recollect the very considerable antipathy towards especially LGBT sexual activities expressed in BDSM shown by cases such as *R v Brown* [1993] UKHL 19.

with clients, including sexual offenders, Mr Pay could not have maintained his clients' respect. Accordingly, the dismissal was justified.

In 2009, in an unfair dismissal case,[27] Professor Fosh had represented a doctoral student at a hearing before the Employment Tribunal. The employer decided to dismiss the Professor and then conducted a search of the Professor's email account. This showed that she had criticised her manager to former students and had helped her doctoral student with a funding bid in the student's name. The Professor was dismissed and brought a claim for unfair dismissal, which failed and lost appeals to the Employment Appeal Tribunal and Court of Appeal. The Professor argued that her case was equivalent to that of Ms Copland, but the EAT disagreed. The search of the Claimant's emails was authorised in accordance with the Respondent's internal rules. Further, the case post-dated the passing of the Regulation of Investigating Powers Act 2000 (RIPA). That legislation was not in force at the time of the matters raised in Ms Copland's complaint.

In *Gayle v Swansea,* Mr Gayle was filmed at a squash court during work hours. The squash court was a private place, but the Court held that the employer's public interest in how its employees use their time was of greater significance than the location.[28]

In *Garamukanwa,* the EAT held that an employee had no expectation of privacy in photographs on his iPhone or in emails sent to a colleague with whom he had had an affair. These activities ceased to be personal when the police investigated him for stalking.[29]

In the High Court case of *Simpkin v Berkeley Group*, an employer asked a senior manager to resign before he could benefit from various company incentive plans. At a preliminary hearing, he sought to exclude from the trial various documents relating to his personal divorce. He said that the documents came into the employer's possession as a result of a private communication. The employer was allowed, however, to rely on the information at trial since, in his contract, his employer had reserved the right to monitor his emails, and the document had been produced on the employer's IT system, using the employer's financial system, and saved on the employer's IT system.[30]

Decisions of the ECtHR have also approved the monitoring of messages sent on Yahoo Messenger during work hours[31] and the practice of filming supermarket workers where those workers had received no warning, but the store had a history of theft, and any employee would have understood monitoring was likely.[32] On the other hand, two university lecturers obtained damages against

27 *Fosh v Cardiff University* [2008] EAT 0412/07 and [2009] EWCA Civ 38.
28 *City and County of Swansea v Gayle* [2013] IRLR 768.
29 *Garamukanwa v Solent* [2016] IRLR 476.
30 *Simpkin v The Berkeley Group Holdings Plc* [2017] 4 WLR 116, paras 32–4.
31 *Barbulescu v Romania* [2017] ECHR 742.
32 *Ribalda v Spain* [2018] ECHR 14.

the government of Montenegro in a case where that state had introduced laws limiting the enabling of official or business premises but only for reasons of safety or to protect data. When a University introduced cameras and placed them in the main amphitheatre, it infringed the rights of the article 8 lecturers, and given that the practice was not justified, the infringement was disproportionate.[33]

One way to understand these cases as a whole is to say that, while most compiling of data by employers[34] is lawful, so long as it is justified, that protection does not apply when a manager pursues a private vendetta. In *Copland*, the manager was using the resources of the business to carry out a process of personal observation which had no utility to the business itself. He wanted to know whether his former partner was in a new sexual relationship.[35] Likewise, in *Halford*, ministers had difficulty justifying the covert surveillance of what was a legitimate Employment Tribunal claim.

A further case which falls into this category of vendetta is the case of Andrea Brown, a serving police officer who had travelled to Barbados with her daughter while on sick leave. The employer approached Virgin Atlantic, the relevant carrier, to obtain information which was then used against Ms Brown in a disciplinary investigation. This was an inappropriate act by the senior police officers, whose powers existed for the purpose of detecting crime, and did not permit the making of these requests in an employment dispute.[36]

"Retro-dismissal"

Since 2008, there have been a number of Tribunal claims arising from the following scenario. An employer decides to terminate an employee's contract. The employer then retrospectively searches the employee's computer. It finds some misconduct by the employee, unknown at the time, and relies on that conduct to justify the dismissal of the employee. The facts of *Fosh*, cited previously, are an example of this kind of dismissal.

In one case, a trade unionist complained about bullying and was referred to Occupational Health. A subsequent trawl of his Facebook account found that several years previously, he had made derogatory comments about his managers and threatened to get drunk at work.[37] The EAT held that his subsequent dismissal was fair.

33 *Antovic and Mirkovic v Montenegro* [2017] ECHR 1068, paras 58–60.

34 Where employees have been involved in covert recording, the admissibility of the evidence gathered by them is addressed in *Vaughan v London Borough of Lewisham and Ors* [2013] EAT 0534/12, paras 12, 26, 29; *Punjab National Bank (International) Ltd and Ors v Gosain* [2014] EAT 0003/14; *Northbay Pelagic Ltd v Anderson* [2021] EAT 00029/18, paras 66–76.

35 The case can sensibly be compared to *Wood v Freeloader Ltd* [1977] IRLR 455: Sexual advances drawing an employee into a relationship. Such behaviour was a repudiatory breach of the relationship between employer and employee, even where the relationship was consensual.

36 *The Commissioner of Police of the Metropolis v Brown* [2018] EWHC 2046, paras 5–9.

37 *British Waterways Board (t/a Scottish Canals) v Smith* [2015] EAT 0004/15.

In a further case, Mr Atkinson was offered a compromised termination with a settlement, which he declined. A subsequent email trawl found that, in breach of the employer's email policy, he had sent sexual emails to his partner from his work email address. It also found that he had coached his partner three years earlier through a job application with the same business. Mr Atkinson resigned and brought a claim of unfair constructive dismissal to the Tribunal, which was dismissed. Mr Atkinson appealed, arguing the emails to his partner had been private. The EAT did not agree:

> To describe reliance by the Respondents on what they had discovered the Claimant to have done, having regard to Article 8, as an unjustified interference with the Claimant's private life when they were legitimately investigating the Claimant's conduct in the circumstances which we have earlier described appears to us to be untenable.[38]

Employment pre-screening

Further, there is a growing phenomenon of using employees' data (for example, employees' social media posts) in pre-hire screening. Various potential remedies are available to limit this practice, including claims under the Equality Act (e.g., claims brought by disabled employees against health questionnaires), blacklisting claims, and claims under sections 137 and 138 Trade Union and Labour Relations (Consolidation) Act 1992, which govern refusals of employment employers or agencies. Section 137 provides:

(1) It is unlawful to refuse a person employment –

  (a) because he is, or is not, a member of a trade union, or
  (b) because he is unwilling to accept a requirement –

    (i) to take steps to become or cease to be, or to remain or not to become, a member of a trade union, or
    (ii) to make payments or suffer deductions in the event of his not being a member of a trade union . . .

(3) Where an advertisement is published which indicates, or might reasonably be understood as indicating –

  (a) that employment to which the advertisement relates is open only to a person who is, or is not, a member of a trade union, or
  (b) that any such requirement as is mentioned in subsection (1)(b) will be imposed in relation to employment to which the advertisement relates, a person who does not satisfy that condition or, as the case

38 *Atkinson v Community Gateway Association* [2014] IRLR 834, para 54.

> may be, is unwilling to accept that requirement, and who seeks and is refused employment to which the advertisement relates, shall be conclusively presumed to have been refused employment for that reason.

There have been relatively few appellate cases on pre-employment screening. In one case, a construction worker was refused employment before he started because of his trade union history. On appeal, the employer argued unsuccessfully that the site manager did not have the authority to refuse offers of work.[39]

In another case, a social worker was refused employment because he had worked for the council previously and had an uncooperative attitude and an anti-management style. A Tribunal initially accepted that this was not discrimination for trade union membership but for his style and attitude. On appeal, its distinction between union membership and activities was found to be untenable, and the case was remitted for a further hearing.[40]

Non-disclosure agreements

Finally, there are a number of cases concerning settled employment, after which journalists seek to inform the public about what took place; however, the parties have reached an agreement to keep the outcome private.

By section 203 Employment Rights Act 1996, an employee may not waive their rights to bring proceedings before an Employment Tribunal except after having made an agreement in writing and received advice from an independent adviser as to the terms and effect of the proposed agreement. The purpose of that clause is to protect employees and to prevent them from signing away their rights in response to offers from their employers which undervalue them. Among the terms commonly found in settlement agreements are non-derogation clauses and confidentiality clauses.

Where the parties agree not to disclose the fact that they have reached a settlement agreement, various article 10 rights are engaged, including the right of the Claimant to express (or, depending on the case, not to express) their opinion as to what happened in the workplace, and the rights of the press to impart information without interference.

Section 12 of the Human Rights Act 1998 applies if a court is considering whether to grant any relief which, if granted, might affect the exercise of the Convention's right to freedom of expression. Sub-section 3 provides that no such relief is to be granted so as to restrain publication before trial unless the Court is satisfied that the applicant is likely to establish that publication should not be allowed. Sub-section 4 provides further matters to which the Court must have particular regard, including the importance of the Convention's right to freedom of expression and whether it is, or would be, in the

39 *Beaver Management Services Ltd v Acheson* [2011] EAT/0268/11.

40 *Harrison v Kent County Council* [1995] ICR 434.

public interest for the material to be published. These provisions operate as a signal to the courts that they should not make orders at preliminary hearings preventing the publication of information where there is a public interest in its content being generally known.

In *ABC and Ors v Telegraph Media Group Ltd*, two businesses and an unnamed senior individual sought to uphold an injunction which had been made restraining the publication of non-disclosure agreements reached following the negotiation of five complaints of sexual harassment, two of which had progressed as far as the issuing of Tribunal claims.

In reaching its decision, the Court of Appeal drew on a Report of the House of Commons Women and Equalities Select Committee entitled *Sexual Harassment in the Workplace*. That document had called on the government to clean up the use of non-disclosure agreements, which, the authors said, "are used unfairly by some employers and also some members of the legal profession to silence victims of sexual harassment". However, the report stopped short of calling for the abolition of such agreements and acknowledged that they sometimes operated to the benefit of Claimants:

> [T]here is a place for NDAs in settlement agreements; there may be times when a victim makes the judgement that signing an NDA is genuinely in their own best interests, perhaps because it provides a route to resolution that they feel would entail less trauma than going to court, or because they value the guarantee of privacy.[41]

The Court refused the appeal and upheld the injunction.[42]

41 *ABC and Ors v Telegraph Media Group Ltd* [2018] EWCA Civ 2329, para 42.
42 *Duchy Farm Kennels Ltd v Steels* [2020] EWHC 1208, paras 66–8.

5 Duties of employers

Specific sectors

The subject of this chapter is the enhanced duties to protect freedom of expression which apply to particular sectors: (i) the public sector as opposed to the private sector, (ii) Higher Education, (iii) Local Government, (iv) schools, and (v) trade unions.

Public and private sector

A number of statutory duties place greater relevant burdens on public rather than private employees. For example, the section 149 duty on employers to give due regard to equality contains in section 149(1)(c) an obligation to:

foster good relations between persons who share a relevant protected characteristic and persons who do not share it.

The most comprehensive guide to a public body's duties was given in the Court of Appeal cases *Bracking*.[1] This guidance provides that

(1) Equality duties are an integral and important part of the mechanisms for ensuring the fulfilment of the aims of anti-discrimination legislation.[2]
(2) An important evidential element in the demonstration of the discharge of the duty is the recording of the steps taken by the decision maker in seeking to meet the statutory requirements.[3]
(3) The relevant duty is upon the Minister or other decision maker personally. What matters is what he or she took into account and what he or she knew. Thus, the Minister or decision maker cannot be taken to know what his or her officials know or what may have been in the minds of officials in proffering their advice.[4]

1 *Bracking v Secretary of State for Work and Pensions* [2013] EWCA Civ 1345.
2 *R (Elias) v Secretary of State for Defence* [2006] EWCA Civ 1293, 274.
3 *R (BAPIO Action Ltd) v Secretary of State for the Home Department* [2007] EWHC 199.
4 *R (National Association of Health Stores) v Department of Health* [2005] EWCA Civ 154, paras 26–7.

DOI: 10.4324/9781032724263-5

(4) A Minister must assess the risk and extent of any adverse impact and the ways in which such risk may be eliminated before the adoption of a proposed policy and not merely as a "rearguard action", following a concluded decision.[5]

(5) (i) The public authority decision maker must be aware of the duty to have "due regard" to the relevant matters;

(ii) The duty must be fulfilled before and at the time when a particular policy is being considered;
(iii) The duty must be "exercised in substance, with rigour, and with an open mind". It is not a question of "ticking boxes"; while there is no duty to make express reference to the regard paid to the relevant duty, reference to it and to the relevant criteria reduces the scope for argument;
(iv) The duty is non-delegable; and
(v) Is a continuing one.
(vi) It is good practice for a decision maker to keep records demonstrating consideration of the duty.[6]

(6) [G]eneral regard to issues of equality is not the same as having specific regard, by way of conscious approach to the statutory criteria.[7]

(7) Officials reporting to or advising Ministers/other public authority decision makers, on matters material to the discharge of the duty, must not merely tell the Minister/decision maker what he/she wants to hear but they have to be "rigorous in both enquiring and reporting to them".[8]

While there have not been cases, to the best of the author's knowledge, in which section 149 has been used in an employment context in relation to religion or belief, the legislation creates the opportunity for a Claimant to bring a case arguing that their public sector employer had failed to give due regard to the need to foster good relations between persons who hold a particular opinion and persons who do not share it.

Higher education

The principle of academic freedom is encapsulated in Recommendation 1762 (2006) of the Parliamentary Assembly of the Council of Europe:

4. In accordance with the Magna Charta Universitatum, the Assembly reaffirms the right to academic freedom and university autonomy which comprises the following principles:

5 *Kaur & Shah v LB Ealing* [2008] EWHC 2062, paras 23–4.
6 *R (Brown) v Secretary of State for Work and Pensions* [2008] EWHC 3158.
7 *R (Meany) v Harlow DC* [2009] EWHC 559, para 84, approved in *R (Bailey) v Brent LBC* [2011] EWCA Civ 1586, paras 74–5.
8 *R (Domb) v Hammersmith & Fulham LBC* [2009] EWCA Civ 941, para 79.

> 4.1 Academic freedom in research and in training should guarantee freedom of expression and of action, freedom to disseminate information and freedom to conduct research and distribute knowledge and truth without restriction . . .
>
> 4.3 History has proven that violations of academic freedom and university autonomy have always resulted in intellectual relapse, and consequently in social and economic stagnation.[9]

Similarly, the UN Committee on Economic, Social and Cultural Rights has stated that:

> Members of the academic community, individually or collectively, are free to pursue, develop and transmit knowledge and ideas, through research, teaching, study, discussion, documentation, production, creating or writing. Academic freedom includes the liberty of individuals to express freely opinions about the institution or system in which they work, to fulfil their functions without discrimination or fear of repression by the State or any other actor, to participate in professional or representative academic bodies, and to enjoy all the internationally recognized human rights applicable to other individuals in the same jurisdiction.[10]

The European Court of Human Rights has stated that academic freedom "should guarantee freedom of expression and of action, freedom to disseminate information and freedom to conduct research and distribute knowledge and truth without restriction".[11]

However, the precise contours of the principle of academic freedom are not resolved and remain contested: "The meaning, rationale and scope of academic freedom are not obvious, as the legal concept is not settled".[12] In *Mustafa Erdogan and Others v Turkey*, for example, three ECtHR judges held that there was a difference between the protection offered to academic speaking on subjects within the sphere of their research and other language, even if that expression took place within a University:

> In determining whether "speech" has an "academic element" it is necessary to establish: (a) whether the person making the speech can be considered an academic; (b) whether that person's public comments or utterances fall within the sphere of his or her research; and (c) whether that person's

9 'Academic Freedom and Autonomy,' Recommendation 1762(2006), Parliamentary Assembly of the Council of Europe, 30 June 2006.

10 General Comment No 13, The Right to Education, Committee on Economic, Social and Cultural Rights, UN Doc E/C.12/1999/10, 8 December 1999, para 39.

11 *Erdogan and Others v Turkey* [2014] ECHR 530, para 40. See, similarly, *Sorguc v Turkey* [2009] ECHR 97, para 35; *Aksu v Turkey* [2012] ECHR 445 para 71.

12 *Erdogan v Turkey*, para 40.

> statements amount to conclusions or opinions based on his or her professional expertise and competence.[13]

Those dicta imply that other forms of expression located in a university context would be denied the heightened protection of academic freedom – for example, events hosted by outside bodies or expression by academics outside the sphere of their research.

In general, human rights caselaw has sought to afford significant protection to academic expression. But to receive this heightened protection, the academic must speak within the bounds of his or her professional expertise. So, in *Erdoğan v Turkey*,[14] a Professor published a piece in an academic law journal criticising senior judges for dissolving a political party and portraying them as incompetent. Erdoğan was writing for an audience of academics and in his specialist area.

By contrast, in 2004, Bruno Gollnisch, a University professor of Japanese and an election candidate for the French far-right party, the Front National, was suspended from teaching in his college after saying at a press conference that there had been no gas chambers in Hitler's concentration camps. Gollnisch was speaking outside his area of academic knowledge. The Court held that his contribution to the spreading of disorder within his university was incompatible with his duties as a teacher. Accordingly, it was found that his suspension had been lawful and there had been no breach of article 10.[15]

Universities and domestic law

Universities are also bound by charity law. As charities, universities must only act in ways which further their objectives. These objects must be for the public benefit (Part 1, Charities Act 2011). A university's trustees must comply with the university's obligations to protect freedom of expression and to protect students, employees, and workers from harassment, discrimination, etc.

Universities are subject to section 43 of the Education (No.2) Act 1986 ("Freedom of speech in universities, polytechnics and colleges") which provides that:

> (1) Every individual and body of persons concerned in the government of any establishment to which this section applies shall take such steps as are reasonably practicable to ensure that freedom of speech within the law is secured for members, students, and employees of the establishment and for visiting speakers.

13 *Erdogan v Turkey*, para 8.

14 *Erdoğan v Turkey*.

15 *Gollnisch v France*, application no 48135/08.

(2) The duty imposed by subsection (1) includes (in particular) the duty to ensure, so far as is reasonably practicable, that the use of any premises of the establishment is not denied to any individual or body of persons on any ground connected with –

(a) the beliefs or views of that individual or of any member of that body; or
(b) the policy or objectives of that body.

Subsections 43(3) and (4) require universities to issue, keep up to date, and apply codes of practice setting out procedures to give effect to this duty.

In the 1991 case of *R v University of Liverpool ex parte Caesar-Gordon*, a University Conservative Association sought and obtained a declaration from the High Court permitting a meeting which was due to be addressed by a diplomat from apartheid South Africa. The University had cancelled the meeting because of fears about public order at the meeting and in the residential area around the university. The Court held that the University had a duty to ensure free speech pursuant to section 43 and was not entitled to take account of threats of public disorder outside the University by persons not within its control.[16]

In 2015, the High Court upheld a decision of Southampton University to withdraw a platform from its own senior academics, days before a conference organised by them was due to take place on the operation of International Law within Israel. HHJ Robinson held that the infringement of the lecturers' rights of expression was proportionate on several grounds including the fact that the cancellation had not extinguished entirely their capacity to hold the event. For example, they could, conceivably, have approached other universities in Britain and found a new venue willing to host the speakers at short notice.[17]

There followed a year of negotiations between the organisers of the intended event and the University, during which the former gave further grounds for the event to go ahead, and the University continued to oppose it. In a second set of judicial review proceedings before the High Court, Whipple J was content to accept the University's assessment that had the conference gone ahead, one or another student group might have protested against it. It was, in any event, for the University and not the High Court to decide which events it permitted and which it decided to cancel.[18]

On occasion, universities have argued that they are excluded from the duties set out in the Human Rights Act. Section 6 Human Rights Act provides that it is unlawful for a public authority to act in a way which is incompatible

16 *R v University of Liverpool ex parte Caesar-Gordon* (1991) 1 QB 124.
17 *R (Ben-Dor) v Abu-Sharkh* [2015] EWHC 2206, para 27.
18 *R (Ben-Dor) v University of Southampton* [2016] EWHC 953.

with a Convention right. Section 6(5) of the Act provides that "a person is not a public authority" if "the nature of the act is private". Certain decisions of universities have been found to be of a private nature: decisions to promote staff,[19] decisions relating to VAT payments,[20] and decisions of newspapers to publish material about a member of the public (where the ultimate source of the information was a university).[21] Quite a large number of cases concerning student sit-ins have proceeded on the assumption that universities are purely private bodies and the Convention Rights do not apply to them.[22]

The argument itself, however, is tenuous, especially given the duties in section 43, and when raised, it should be challenged. It would be extraordinary if Universities had no Convention duties to protect free speech despite having extensive legislative and public duties, fixed by Parliament, of exactly this character.

Higher education (Freedom of Speech) Act 2023

The duty ("the section 43 duty") has been augmented by the Higher Education (Freedom of Speech) Act 2023. That Act imposed duties on higher education providers to protect freedom of speech for staff, students, other members of the university, and visiting speakers.[23] Students' unions were also placed under a similar duty.[24]

The Office for Students was given the power to find that a governing body or students' union had breached its duties to protect expression.[25]

A new section A6 of the Higher Education and Research Act 2017 created a civil right for staff, members of universities, students, and visiting speakers to sue universities and students' unions if they did not uphold freedom of expression. That right could only be exercised, however, if the person intending to sue had first of all complained to the university concerned or to the Office for Students.

A number of other changes were made in the Act. It introduced, for example, a new requirement that where a university negotiated a non-disclosure agreement, that agreement could not prohibit the complainant from raising in

19 *Evans v The University of Cambridge* [2002] EWHC 1382, para 13.

20 *The Chancellor, Master & Scholars of the University of Cambridge v HMRC* [2009] EWHC 4343, para 47.

21 *Piepenbrock v London School of Economics and Political Science* [2022] EWHC 2421 (KB), paras 209–10.

22 *School of Oriental and African Studies v Persons Unknown* [2010] EWHC 3977 paras 20–8; *University of Manchester and Others v Persons Unknown* (unreported) 20 March 2023, paras 13–14; *University of Sussex v Persons Unknown* [2013] EWHC 862.

23 Section A1 Higher Education and Research Act 2017.

24 Section A4 Higher Education and Research Act 2017.

25 Section 69C Higher Education and Research Act 2017.

public the fact that they had complained about sexual abuse, misconduct or harassment, or other bullying or harassment.[26]

Political neutrality clauses in local government and outside

The Local Government Officers (Political Restrictions) Regulations 1990 place limitations on the ability of employees holding politically restricted posts to engage in party-political activity. Reg 3 of those regulations make it an implied term of every such post-holder's role that they will not be a candidate for election to a local authority, the House of Commons, or the European Parliament; that they shall not act as an agent or sub-agent for such a candidate; that they shall not be an officer of a political party; and they shall not canvass on behalf of a party. The Regulations also restrict what officers may do to speak or write on behalf of parties.

Section 5 of the Constitutional Reform and Governance Act 2010 places an obligation of political neutrality on civil servants.

On the other hand, it is arguable that a neutrality clause cannot be given effect unless it is not necessary for the employment. Section 203(1) Employment Rights Act 1996 voids any term of employment which is inconsistent with the rights conferred by that Act, and it is at least arguable that this section voids neutrality clauses where there is nothing about the employment which actually requires or justifies them.[27]

Local government: other issues

Local government officers have wide powers to prosecute offences, including for environmental, licensing, planning, waste, and welfare benefits offences. Sometimes, a local government prosecutor will prosecute fellow council employees. It is plausible that there might be a discriminatory purpose behind those actions. In *London Borough of Waltham Forest v Martin*, the EAT held that when an employer is carrying out functions as a public prosecutor, those functions are outside the employment sphere. In other words, while the County Court does have jurisdiction to hear claims in relation to discriminatory prosecution decisions, the Employment Tribunal has no power to hear them.[28]

26 Section A1(11) Higher Education and Research Act 2017.

27 These clauses were considered, albeit without their meaning being resolved, in *Scottish Federation of Housing Associations v Jones* [2022] EAT 114, paras 25–7.

28 *London Borough of Waltham Forest v Martin* [2011] EAT 0069/11, para 21. The same applies in whistleblowing cases: *Tiplady v City of Bradford* [2019] EWCA Civ 2180, para 45.

In Chapter 3, we saw that employer justifications for limiting free speech are often connected to the supposed reputational damage done by employees. It is at least arguable that there can be no legitimate aim in protecting the reputation of a local authority. Such an authority cannot maintain an action for damages in defamation.[29] A local authority is a governmental body; it is elected, and it is thus of the highest public importance that it should be open to uninhibited criticism. It has been argued in employment proceedings that the same principles apply to ordinary dismissals where a local authority dismisses for the reason of loss of reputation, i.e., that since a local council cannot sue for libel, neither can it invoke the principle of reputational damage. While the EAT did not address that argument directly, and it remains to be tested in future litigation, the Appeal Tribunal did find that (even if true) such an argument could not be extended to other bodies which are subject to local authority control, such as schools, whose leading members are not elected.[30]

Schools

Local authority-run schools are subject to the Education Act 1996. Chapter III of the Act sets out various duties of local authorities to promote high standards, ensure fair access to opportunities for education and training, and promote the fulfilment of learning potential by every pupil. Section 109 of the Education And Skills Act 2008 gives the Chief Inspector of Schools, exercised via Ofsted, a duty to inspect schools and report. This duty is applied pursuant to a framework, presently the "Education Inspection Framework". Both schools themselves and, indeed, Ofsted are subject to the Public Sector Equality Duty set out in section 149 of the Equality Act 2010 (see Chapter 2).

Independent schools are bound by the Education (Independent School Standards) Regulations 2014 ("the ISSR"). Paragraph 2 of the Schedule to the ISSR provides:

(1) The standard in this paragraph is met if –

- (a) the proprietor ensures that a written policy on the curriculum, supported by appropriate plans and schemes of work, which provides for the matters specified in sub-paragraph (2) is drawn up and implemented effectively; and
- (b) the written policy, plans, and schemes of work–
  - (i) take into account the ages, aptitudes, and needs of all pupils, including those pupils with an EHC plan; and

29 *Derbyshire County Council v Times Newspapers* [1993] AC534.
30 *Hill v Governing Body of Great Tey Primary School* [2013] EAT 0237/12, para 61.

(ii) do not undermine the fundamental British values of democracy, the rule of law, individual liberty, and mutual respect and tolerance of those with different faiths and beliefs.

Paragraph 5 of the Schedule to the ISSR provides that schools must meet a standard for the delivery of the spiritual, moral, social, and cultural development of pupils:

> The standard about the spiritual, moral, social, and cultural development of pupils at the school is met if the proprietor –
>
> (a) actively promotes the fundamental British values of democracy, the rule of law, individual liberty, and mutual respect and tolerance of those with different faiths and beliefs;
> (b) ensures that principles are actively promoted which . . .
>
> (v) further tolerance and harmony between different cultural traditions by enabling pupils to acquire an appreciation of and respect for their own and other cultures;
> (vi) encourage respect for other people, paying particular regard to the protected characteristics set out in the 2010 Act . . .

Failure to apply the Regulations can result in regulatory or enforcement action against the school by the Secretary of State. The Department for Education ("DfE") produces guidance to accompany the ISSR which explains:

> Inspectors will take this guidance into account when reporting to the Secretary of State on the extent to which the independent school standards are being met, or are likely to be met, in relation to an independent school. . . . The Secretary of State has also signalled that he will be taking a firmer approach to enforce the standards when there is evidence of non-compliance. This is reflected in the policy statement on regulatory and enforcement action which is published alongside this guidance. All of the standards are mandatory and should be met by independent schools at all times except where they do not apply to particular types of school.[31]

The ISSR were cited in the first instance case of *Randall v Trent College*, which concerned a High Church Anglican chaplain who had delivered a series of sermons to pupils to the effect that "it is sinful to alter the body given by God, implied that marriage can only be between a man and a woman, and that family works best when a woman, with her tone of voice, looks after the children". Part of the reason these opinions proved controversial within the school

31 Schedule 2, regulation 5, Education (Independent School Standards) Regulations 2014.

was that they were presented in Church to young pupils – a captive audience bound by silence – as the unanswerable opinion of the Christian religion. The Chaplain was dismissed in 2019 (although reinstated, before being subsequently dismissed a second time, this time for reason of redundancy). The Tribunal found that the reason for that dismissal was not his beliefs. Rather, "the time, the place, to whom he expressed his beliefs and the manner in which he expressed them" caused his dismissal.[32]

In order to provide child-care provision for what are termed early years providers, which covers children up to reception age, or later years children, who are children up to the age of 8, or those who manage such providers, which will include head teachers, an individual teacher or head teacher must be registered. But, certain categories of persons are disqualified from registration unless they have specific permission. Disqualified persons include those who have committed serious violent offences, sexual offences, and offences against children. They also include persons who either live in the same household where a disqualified person lives, or in a household where such a person is employed.[33]

The employer sought to rely on these provisions in the case of *A v B Local Authority*, which concerned a primary school headteacher who had had a close personal friendship with a man who was convicted of making indecent images of children by downloading them onto his computer. The teacher was found to have been unfairly dismissed. The school appealed the finding of unfair dismissal and was successful at the Court of Appeal. Lady Justice Black and Lord Justice Floyd found that, on the facts, the headteacher had an overriding obligation to report her friend's conviction.[34]

Trade unions and professional associations

Section 57 Equality Act 2010 brings trade organisations within the coverage of the Act. The definition of trade organisation, contained in the same section, is very broad and intended to encompass all trade bodies and not merely trade unions:

(7) A trade organisation is –

  (a) an organisation of workers,
  (b) an organisation of employers, or
  (c) any other organisation whose members carry on a particular trade or profession for the purposes for which the organisation exists.

In addition to the many cases involving the speech of trade unionists, which have been cited throughout the body of this book, there have been

32 *Randall v Trent College Limited* [2023] WL 02374347, paras 56, 78, 257, 295.
33 Reg 9, Childcare (Disqualification) Regulations 2009.
34 *A v B Local Authority and Anor* [2016] EWCA Civ 766, para 18.

cases where members of unions have been in dispute with their trade union and have sought to challenge the quantity or quality of resources provided to them or the decisions made by unions. For example, in *D'Silva v NATFHE*, a member of an education union was advised by a barrister instructed by the union to withdraw parts of his case. Mr D'Silva then brought proceedings to the Tribunal and, on appeal, to the Employment Appeal Tribunal, saying that he had been unfavourably treated on grounds of his race. His claim failed on its facts.[35]

In *GMB v Allen*,[36] a group of local government workers complained that their trade union had settled equal pay claims on terms unfavourable to them. The decision that this amounted to discrimination was overturned by the EAT but upheld by the Court of Appeal. The central issue in the litigation was whether the union had misled its members. The Tribunal, having found that it had, the Court of Appeal held that the means were disproportionate and that the resulting indirect discrimination on grounds of sex was unjustified.

In *UNITE v Nailard*, the appeal courts considered a trade union's liability for acts of bullying and harassment carried out against one of its (employed) regional officers by its (lay) officials. The Tribunal held that the acts took place on grounds of sex. The union disputed that it was liable for the conduct of its lay officials, or at least for such conduct when it was directed against an employed officer of the union. The Court rejected that analysis and found that unions were liable.[37]

There are occasions when trade unions are given confidential information by their members. The difficulty for the trade unionists is that they have no protection under the whistleblowing legislation. And if they make use of the information in their trade union activities, they risk detriment or dismissal for doing so. In *Morris v Metrolink*, the Court of Appeal considered a trade unionist who was shown a part of a manager's diary, which appeared to prove that they had breached the company's rules. The trade unionist revealed that document and was dismissed. The Court of Appeal found the dismissal unfair.[38]

35 *D'Silva v NATFHE and Ors* [2008] EAT 0384/07.

36 *Allen and Ors v GMB* [2008] EWCA Civ 810.

37 *Unite the Union v Nailard* [2018] EWCA Civ 1203.

38 *Morris v Metrolink RATP Dev Ltd* [2018] EWCA Civ 1358, para 39.

6 Competing appeals to non-discrimination rules

The subject of this chapter is conflicts between two groups of people in the workplace, with members of one group campaigning for people in another group to be sanctioned on grounds of their expression. In this scenario, a group of employees or customers believe that their access to the business is compromised by expression which infringes their dignity, i.e., because a member of staff has expressed language which amounts to the harassment of a protected group of people contrary to the Equality Act. When an employee's language has, or has arguably, been harassment so as to satisfy Section 26 Equality Act 2010, the problem facing employers is that they have, at first sight, *two* groups of people, each demanding the protection of the same Act.

Competing rights under the Convention

Structured into the Convention is the idea that every expression of opinion is a qualified right. The individual is always perceived as being in relationship to society as a whole. So, in *Sánchez v Spain*, the ECtHR considered whether there had been a breach of Article 10 in circumstances where employees who were on the executive of the relevant trade union and had brought proceedings against their employer for union recognition, were dismissed for publishing a newsletter containing an offensive cartoon depicting a manager and two co-workers who had testified against the union in the previous recognition proceedings.

The Spanish courts dismissed their complaints of a violation of freedom of expression, considering the restriction to be justified. The Court held that the Spanish courts were required to balance the applicants' right to freedom of expression "against the right to honour and dignity" of the three impugned colleagues, who had been represented in an offensive and gratuitous manner.[1]

Article 10 protects both "receiv[ing]" and "impart[ing]" information. A number of decisions of the ECtHR grasp that an audience has rights.

1 *Sánchez v Spain* [2011] IRLR 934.

DOI: 10.4324/9781032724263-6

Freedom can also serve to protect those who are heckling or taking part in speech acts of their own. Cases in which freedom of expression has been found to protect those speaking out against another person have included *Steel and ors v United Kingdom*,[2] which concerned the rights of protesters handing out leaflets with the intention of undermining the publicity campaign of a large multinational business, and *Handzhiyski v Bulgaria*,[3] where a protest took the form of placing a Santa Claus cap and a red bag on the statue of a political figure, in order to embarrass that rival.

Competing rights under the Act

In scenarios of competing appeals to the Equality Act, the structure of analysis is different from what it is in the Convention. Any analysis under the Act must reduce what may well have been three-sided conflicts (disputes between two groups of people in the workplace, with the employer choosing which of the contending groups to support) to two-sided conflicts, disputes solely between the employer and the employee.

With claims of direct discrimination, harassment, or victimisation, because there is no justification defence, the courts cannot find that an employer discriminated against an employee and that they were right to do so.

Conflicts between LGBT people and religious groups: positive action

At one time, it seemed likely that the law would give a very wide discretion to religious bodies and favour their interests generally against LGBT people.

So, when the original Regulations protecting against discrimination on the grounds of religion or belief were made in 2003, ministers drafted them to give religious bodies an opportunity to invoke the principle of positive action. Regulation 7(2) provided that employers would not be guilty of discrimination where they acted "to avoid conflicting with the strongly held religious convictions of a significant number of the religion's followers".[4]

The Regulations were subject to a judicial review in 2004, with seven trade unions complaining that the regulations went too far in terms of protecting religious organisations from discrimination complaints. The High Court upheld the Regulations.[5]

Similarly, in *Pemberton v Inwood*, the principle of positive action was successfully invoked by the Church of England when the Claimant was refused

2 *Steel and ors v United Kingdom* [2011] ECHR 2272.
3 *Handzhiyski v Bulgaria* (2021) 73 EHRR 15.
4 A broadly-similar power is now contained in Schedule 9 paragraph 2 of the Equality Act 2010.
5 *Amicus MSF Section*, para 80.

an Extra Parochial Ministry Licence, meaning he could not be appointed to the post of Chaplaincy and Bereavement Manager in a Faith Centre run by an NHS Trust. Lady Justice Asplin concluded her decision by remarking that she could understand why Canon Pemberton must find the Church of England's official stance to be wrong but that it was no violation of his dignity that those rules had been applied, however wrong he believed them to be: "Not all opposition of interests is hostile or offensive".[6] On the other hand, as we have seen already in the case of *Randall v Trent College* (Chapter 5), there have now been a very large number of cases where Christian employees were found to have been fairly dismissed or where claims of discrimination failed after they sought to make converts in the workplace.

Muslims around 9/11

With the making of the 2003 regulations outlawing discrimination on grounds of religion or belief, the single most important people to acquire protection were Muslims. A series of decisions had already brought Jews[7] and Sikhs[8] within the protection of race laws. As soon as the Regulations were made, leading academic lawyers' voices could be heard asking whether the protection or religion was really needed.[9]

Both in the UK and, indeed, in Europe, the judiciary has shown a very marked reluctance to uphold the right of Muslims to wear clothing associated with their religion, principally the Islamic headscarf. So, for example, in *Dahlab v Switzerland* (a pre-9/11 case), the European Court of Human Rights accepted the argument made by the Swiss authorities that the veil was a "powerful external symbol", which, if worn in front of a mixed-class of Muslim and Christian children, would have a "proselytising effect" on the latter, so that in order to prevent their parents from being offended, and in order to uphold the school's message of "tolerance", it was necessary to ban Muslims from wearing it.[10]

Similarly, in *Sahin v Turkey*,[11] the ECtHR held a Turkish university had acted proportionately in denying access to lectures to a medical student who wore a veil on the grounds that the veil was not merely a symbol of religious belief but also of political affiliation, and the state was entitled to prohibit opinions with which it disagreed.[12]

6 *Pemberton v Inwood* [2018] EWCA Civ 564, paras 61–2.
7 *Seide v Gillette Industries Limited* [1980] IRLR 427.
8 *Mandla (Sewa Singh) v Dowell Lee* (1983) 2 AC 548.
9 A. McColgan, *Discrimination, Equality and the Law* (Oxford: Hart, 2016), p 67; A. McColgan, *Equality Act 2010* (London: Institute of Employment Rights, 2011), pp 44–5.
10 *Dahlab v Switzerland* [2001] ECHR 15.
11 *Sahin v Turkey* (2007) 44 EHRR 5.
12 We will see later in this chapter that the ECtHR, when faced with deciding whether to protect comparable physical symbols such as the Christian cross, has taken a much more permissive approach.

In the domestic case of *Azmi v Kirklees*,[13] the EAT considered the case of a bilingual support worker in a primary school who was dismissed for refusing to remove a face veil (a niqab) when teaching students. The employer argued that under its dress code, all facial coverings were unlawful. The Employment Tribunal held that Ms Azmi should be compared to a teacher who attended school in a motorcycle helmet and refused to take it off on request. They would have been fairly dismissed, and Ms Azmi's dismissal was fair.

The decision has been controversial ever since. People who grow up in religious communities are expected to follow the norms of the people around them in terms of language, food, and dress. Those behaviours do not infringe on the dignity of anyone else. Moreover, they have no counterpart in secular society. We do not, in general, require Claimants in direct discrimination cases to supply a comparator. If we did, it would be a matter of genuine difficulty coming up with something equivalent which the secular or Christian employee faces a similar communal encouragement to wear.

There is, moreover, a very striking contrast between the decision and the approach of the High Court towards education cases, where blanket policies banning jewellery have been found to indirectly discriminate against Sikh pupils, for example, who are prevented from wearing the Kara.[14] Putting these cases side by side, it is hard not to feel that the implicit distinction on which the caselaw rests is between an unexplored idea of good religions which require protection (Christianity, Sikhism, Judaism) and other religions which don't.

In the mid-2010s and early 2020s, it seemed that the Court of Justice might inch towards taking a position which was less permissive towards veil bans than that of UK domestic law. In *Bougnaoui v Micropole SA*, the CJEU held that the employer could not defend a veil ban in relation to a claim of direct discrimination by saying that it was a genuine occupational requirement to operate such a ban, where the only evidence for its need was that one of the customers of an IT design business had said that seeing Muslim women wearing a bandana when she visited his workplace made him feel embarrassed.[15]

Bougnaoui was followed up by the case of *WABE*, a worker in a childcare centre who attended the workplace wearing a headscarf; the Court required an employer to produce cogent evidence to show that a ban on all religious clothing was justified.[16]

13 *Azmi v Kirklees Metropolitan Borough Council* [2007] IRLR 484.

14 *Watkins-Singh, R (on the application of) v Aberdare Girls' High School & Anor* [2008] EWHC 1865.

15 *Bougnaoui and ADDH* [2017] IRLR 447, paras 17, 40.

16 *WABE eV and MH Müller Handels GmbH v MJ* [2021] IRLR 832, paras 84–5. There has been some discussion as to whether the decision in *Commune d'Ans* [2023] EUECJ C-148/22 rows back from the previous requirement of justification. On my reading of para 41 of that judgment, the requirement of justification (or necessity) remains in play. Others have read the decision differently.

The best we can say is perhaps that, at the level of EU anti-discrimination, there is an increasingly obvious contradiction between the prohibition of discrimination and the treatment of individuals who seek to manifest their religion by wearing the veil.

Anyone expecting the CJEU to guide the UK courts towards a place of principle is unlikely to be satisfied any time soon.

The silent far-right activist

In the case of *Norwood v United Kingdom*, which had already been cited in Chapter 1, Mr Norwood was a member of the British National Party who displayed a poster inviting attacks on Muslims. He was prosecuted and convicted, and the European Court of Human Rights upheld his conviction pursuant to art 10(2). His treatment seemed to belong to a very long line of cases in which the Court had declined to uphold the rights of racists, Holocaust deniers, and people nostalgic for fascism. Other cases which are seemingly similar to Mr Norwood's have resulted, however, in different outcomes, for example, *Redfearn v the United Kingdom*,[17] where a BNP candidate was dismissed from his post as a bus driver, and the ECtHR found that his art 10 rights had been wrongly infringed.

That case began when the recognised trade union Unison wrote to Mr Redfearn's employer, Serco, complaining about the company's decision to employ him and raising its members' fears of racial hatred. Unison's objection to Mr Redfearn's employment was solely on the fact that he had stood for the BNP during elections and that his presence would dismay co-workers and customers. There was no suggestion that Mr Redfearn had organised in his workplace or said or done anything untoward there. Mr Redfearn was dismissed.

At the Employment Tribunal, Redfearn argued his dismissal had been indirectly discriminatory on grounds of race, reasoning that membership of the BNP was limited to whites[18] and that by imposing a requirement that members of that party could not work for Serco, the company was imposing on its staff a requirement which every black employee could satisfy but a proportion of its white staff could not. It was discriminating indirectly, in other words, against whites, and the discrimination could not be justified.

The Employment Tribunal rejected Mr Redfearn's claim in forthright terms. He appealed, and the Employment Appeal Tribunal ruled in Redfearn's favour. At the Court of Appeal, Lord Justice Mummery held that equality law had not been implemented in order to protect someone accused of being a discriminator:

> Taken to its logical conclusion [Mr Redfearn's] interpretation of the 1976 Act would mean that it could be an act of direct race discrimination for an

17 *Redfearn v the United Kingdom* [2012] ECHR 1878.
18 *Serco Ltd v Redfearn* [2006] ICR 1367, CA, para 16.

> employer, who was trying to improve race relations in the workplace, to dismiss an employee, whom he discovered had committed an act of race discrimination, such as racist abuse, against a fellow employee or against a customer of the employer. I am confident that that is not the kind of case for which the anti-discrimination legislation was designed.[19]

The ECtHR upheld Mr Redfearn's complaint. There had been no objections made to his conduct in the workplace. No consideration had been given to transferring him to a non-customer-facing role. The Court held that, although the Race Relations Act was "not primarily intended to cover a situation such as the present one", the courts should have given the Act "a liberal interpretation" to protect him.[20]

A very different outcome was reached in the 2023 first instance case of *Cave v Open University*. There, a project co-ordinator who lacked the two years' continuous service to have unfair dismissal rights resigned from a university post, claiming to have been constructively dismissed for holding English Nationalist opinions. When asked what those were, he explained that he regarded Jewish and black people as, essentially, not English. Priority in housing, etc., should be given to white English people. He had not discussed his opinions at work, nor had he proselytised on their behalf. His opinions were found to be in clear breach of article 17, and his discrimination claim was struck out.[21]

Gender critical feminists

Forstater v CGD Europe, concerned a tax specialist who had worked for several years as a consultant, found that her contract was not renewed and blamed her employer, the Center for Global Development, for the non-renewal of her contract, arguing that the business had refused her employment because for several months she had been speaking out on social media against proposed measures which would have made it easier for trans people to be recognised in law, and against trans people.

In so far as human rights law prohibits discrimination on grounds of religion or belief, it does so, amongst other things, by restricting protection to beliefs which are compatible with human dignity and the fundamental rights of others.

As far as Ms Forstater was concerned, the question of a person's sex was for her and no one else to decide. She considered that if a transwoman said she was a woman, that statement was untrue, even if that person had a Gender Recognition Certificate. She believed there were two sexes, male and female,

19 *Serco v Redfearn*, paras 43–4.

20 *Redfearn v UK*, para 51.

21 *Cave v Open University*, ET case no 3313198/2020, para 46; also *Thomas v Surrey and Borders Partnership NHS Foundation Trust and Ms A Brett* [2021] ET case no 2304056/2018, although that decision was under appeal at the time this book was written.

there was no spectrum in sex, and there were no circumstances whatsoever under which a person could change from one sex to another or to being of neither sex. She said she would generally seek to be polite to trans persons and would usually seek to respect their choice of pronoun but would not feel bound to. If a trans person who was not assigned female at birth was in a space that was intended to be for women only, then Ms Forstater would object to her presence. In Ms Forstater's opinion, the words man and woman described a person's sex at birth and were immutable. A person was either one or the other; there was nothing else in between, and it was impossible to change from one sex to the other.[22]

Further, Ms Forstater had a practice of regularly interacting with trans people online in a fashion that was likely to upset and antagonise them. For example, in relation to Pips Bunce, a senior director at Credit Suisse who describes themselves as being "gender fluid" and "non-binary", Forstater said, "Bunce does not 'masquerade as female' he is a man who likes to express himself part of the week by wearing a dress". She also wrote, "Bunce is a white man who likes to dress in women's clothes".

The Employment Tribunal found that such opinions required Ms Forstater to cause distress to other people. So, while Ms Forstater considered herself a polite person willing to accede to other people's requests, the reality was that she sought out trans women and made a point of referring to them as men.[23]

Employment Judge Tayler concluded that Ms Forstater's beliefs were likely to manifest themselves in behaviour causing undue distress to others.

> The human rights balancing exercise goes against the Claimant because of the absolutist approach she adopts.[24]

On appeal, the Employment Appeal Tribunal held that in deciding whether a belief is worthy of respect, the courts should apply the same test as under Article 17; in other words, any opinion is protected under the Equality Act so long as it falls short of "challeng[ing] the very notion of democracy" or "destroying the rights of others".[25]

Choudhury P, as he then was, continued,

> It is only those beliefs that would be an affront to Convention principles in a manner akin to that of pursuing totalitarianism, or advocating Nazism, or espousing violence and hatred in the gravest of forms, that should be capable of being not worthy of respect in a democratic society. Beliefs that are offensive, shocking or even disturbing to others, and which fall

22 *Forstater v CGD Europe and others*, ET case no 2200909/2019, para 77.
23 *Forstater v CGD* (2019) ET, para 35.
24 *Forstater v CGD*, para 91.
25 *Forstater v CGD Europe and Ors* [2021] EAT 0105/20, para 59.

> into the less grave forms of hate speech would not be excluded from the protection.[26]

Ms Forstater's views were likely to be unwelcome to trans people but did not have the effect of destroying trans' people's rights altogether. The outcome of that case was that Ms Forstater's opinions were protected under the Equality Act. She could not be dismissed or suffer detriment because of them.

The decision of the Employment Appeal Tribunal in *Forstater* was subject to press scrutiny, with many trans people and sympathetic discrimination lawyers fearing that it would lead to a rapid diminution of trans rights.[27] After all, when we speak about characteristics which are protected under the Equality Act, "gender critical feminism" is unique in that what is being protected is specifically a belief system whose upholders campaign for legal restrictions on trans people. This makes gender-critical opinion a fundamentally different kind of belief system from atheism, pacifism, veganism, socialism, and the other secular beliefs which have been protected under the Act.

Towards the end of its decision, the EAT reminded itself of the distinction between the holding of beliefs, which was protected, and manifesting them:

> The Claimant is subject to same prohibitions on discrimination, victimisation and harassment under the [Equality Act] as the rest of society. Should it be found that her misgendering on a particular occasion, because of its gratuitous nature or otherwise, amounted to harassment of a trans person (or of anyone else for that matter), then she could be liable for such conduct under the [Act].[28]

The difference between beliefs and their manifestations has become the battleground in many of the cases relating to gender-critical opinions. So, for example, in *Forstater* itself, following the appeal to the Appeal Tribunal, the Claimant's case was remitted back for hearing at the first instance where she succeeded. The Tribunal found that the reason Ms Forstater was not offered employment was because of her opinions. It then assessed the proportionality of the infringement of her article 10 right to expression and found that the non-renewal of her contract had not struck a fair balance between her rights and the rights of the community and that direct discrimination was established.[29]

Another gender-critical activist, the barrister Alison Bailey, brought a claim relying on her beliefs, which were that "a woman is defined by her

26 *Forstater v CGD*, EAT, para 79.

27 R. M. White and N. Newbegin, *A Practical Guide to Transgender Law* (London: Law Brief Publishing, May 2021); A. Sharpe, *'Not a Nazi . . . But': Forstater v CGD Europe Critical* (London: Legal Thinking, 29 June 2021).

28 *Forstater v CGD* (EAT, 2021), para 104.

29 *Forstater v CGD Europe and others* [2022] ET claim 2200909/2019, paras 315–16.

sex. She disagrees with the beliefs of those who say that a woman is defined by her gender, which may differ from her sex, and is for the individual to identify". She succeeded around the same time in a Tribunal claim against her chambers, Garden Court, the ET finding that in tweeting the news that it was investigating Ms Bailey's conduct, her chambers had victimised her. She failed, however, in a claim against the LGBT charity Stonewall.[30]

Jo Phoenix succeeded in a claim of unfair dismissal and direct discrimination against her employer, the Open University.[31]

Meanwhile, in *Lister v New College Swindon,* the Employment Tribunal upheld a dismissal, where a Claimant's gender-critical beliefs were manifested in not referring to a pupil by the correct pronouns and in making homophobic tweets. Lister's dismissal was a reasonable response to the complaints made against him by both pupils and colleagues. In particular, the fact that Lister said he would not have changed his behaviour had a less serious sanction been applied played an important part in why the dismissal was justified.[32]

In the civil case of *Sanchez v University of Bristol*,[33] a gender-critical activist complained that she had been harassed by the supporters of trans rights and that the University failed to protect her. HHJ Ralton, sitting in the County Court, rejected the Claimant's claim. He considered that the University did not owe the Claimant a duty of care; if it did, the duty had not been breached and that, in any event, the University was not responsible. The judge also rejected Ms Sanchez's Equality Act claims. Ms Sanchez's most striking allegation was that the University had orchestrated a suspension of her PhD course with the intention of invalidating her scholarship and forcing her to leave. The Court found no basis to support her belief that the suspension was punitive or intended to trick her.

In another civil case, *Ali v Green Party of England and Wales*, the Claimant claimed discrimination based on his gender-critical views for being removed as a spokesperson for the Green Party. HHJ Hellman was careful to specify that it was not discriminatory for a political party merely to remove a spokesperson on the grounds of belief, provided it follows a fair procedure in doing so. He stated,

> The Green Party could not, in any event, have been compelled to maintain Dr Ali as a spokesperson if (outside of a party election period) he expressed beliefs that were inconsistent with Party policy, or if they

30 *Bailey v Stonewall Equality Ltd and others* [2022] ET claim 2202172/2020. At the time of writing, Bailey's appeal against Stonewall is pending judgment at the EAT.

31 *Phoenix v The Open University and others* [2024] ET case nos 3322700/2021 and 3323841/2021. Another example of a gender critical feminist winning a free speech claim at first instance is *Fahmy v Arts Council* [2023] ET case no 6000042/2022.

32 *New College Swindon* [2024] ET case no 1404223/2022.

33 *Sanchez v University of Bristol* [2022] County Court claim no 008LR988.

> reasonably concluded that he would do so, as this would infringe their article 9(10 rights by obliging them to manifest a belief which they did not hold.[34]

The non-binary barrister Oscar Davies has pointed out some of the difficulties of the preset law.

> The framing of a "gender critical" belief as solely "sex is immutable" conveniently omits gender. However, if the belief leads to manifestations such as "transwomen are men", the belief elides sex and gender such that the actual belief seems to be "sex is immutable . . . and gender does not exist/is not important/trans people are lying". It is one thing to say you cannot change your (natal) sex; it is another to say that you cannot change your gender. At the core of many gender-critical beliefs seems to be a paternalistic prerogative seeking to strip people of their rights of self-definition, where a gender critical person may self-define their sex/gender, but a trans person may not. In essence that a transgender person has no right to claim any aspect of the gender that they live in.[35]

The present state of the law leaves employers in an impossible position. The effect of the decisions is that if an individual A harasses B with behaviour which infringes on their dignity, but so long as A's behaviour has a connection (nexus) to an opinion and also A's opinion is not so bad as to be totalitarianism/Nazism, then there is nothing the employer can do. If it doesn't investigate, B has a viable Tribunal claim against the employer. If it does investigate, A has a viable Tribunal claim against the employer. There is literally nothing the employer can do to escape legal liability to one of those two parties.

Other anti-trans activists

In another employment case, *Mackereth v Department for Work and Pensions*, an anti-trans activist who was motivated not by gender-critical feminist belief but by Christian opinion was hostile towards trans people. He believed in the truth of Genesis 1:27, from which it followed that a person could not change their sex/gender at will, and attempting to do so was pointless, self-destructive, and sinful. He did not believe in "gender fluidity".[36] He believed, further, that

34 *Ali v Green Party of England and Wales*, County Court claim no J00CL858, para 243.

35 O. Davies, 'Why the "Gender Critical" Cases Are Bad Law,' *New Law Journal*, 26 April 2024.

36 A characteristic which had been protected in *Taylor v Jaguar* (2020) 9 WLUK 200, ET case no 1304471/2018, para 178: "We thought it was very clear that Parliament intended gender reassignment to be a spectrum moving away from birth sex, and that a person could be at any point on that spectrum. That would be so, whether they described themselves as 'non-binary' i.e. not

it would be irresponsible and dishonest for a health professional to accommodate/encourage a patient's "impersonation" of the opposite sex.

On appeal, Mr Mackereth persuaded the EAT that his beliefs should have been treated as protected. In other words, the set of anti-trans employees who are protected by law is wider than mere gender-critical activists and also extends to include people whose opinions of trans people are purely negative and reactive.

However, when Mr Mackereth resigned from the respondent, his employer had not made a final decision on dismissal; in other words, his dismissal had been self-inflicted.[37] He had not been discriminated against or unfairly dismissed.

The "Reason Why"

Almost all attempts to carve out exceptions to the Equality Act by arguing that one or another group does not deserve the protection of that Act have failed.

That does not mean, at all, that in competing appeals to the Equality Act every claim of direct discrimination must succeed.

The dividing line, in practice, has been that not all warnings or dismissals of a person with a protected characteristic are *because of* that person's characteristic. In practice, the question of why exactly the employer took the challenged decision has become the point on which almost all such cases turn.

This distinction has been affirmed in many cases, not least including by Underhill LJ in *Page v NHS Trust Development Authority*:

> In a direct discrimination claim the essential question is whether the act complained of was done because of the protected characteristic, or, to put the same thing another way, whether the protected characteristic was the reason for it. . . . It is thus necessary in every case properly to characterise the putative discriminator's reason for acting. In the context of the protected characteristic of religion or belief the EAT case-law has recognised a distinction between (1) the case where the reason is the fact that the claimant holds and/or manifests the protected belief, and (2) the case where the reason is that the claimant had manifested that belief in some particular way to which objection could justifiably be taken. In the latter case it is the objectionable manifestation of the belief, and not the belief

at point A or point Z, 'gender fluid' i.e. at different places between point A and point Z at different times, or 'transitioning' i.e. moving from point A, but not necessarily ending at point Z, where A and Z are biological sex. We concluded that it was beyond any doubt that somebody in the situation of the Claimant was (and is) protected by the legislation because they are on that spectrum and they are on a journey which will not be the same in any two cases. It will end up where it does".

37 *Mackereth* [2022] EAT 99, para 124.

> itself, which is treated as the reason for the act complained of. Of course, if the consequences are not such as to justify the act complained of, they cannot sensibly be treated as separate from an objection to the belief itself.[38]

In *Wasteney v East London NHS Foundation Trust*, the Employment Appeal Tribunal considered the cases of a senior Christian employee who was accused of having subjected a Muslim subordinate to unwanted and unwelcome conduct, including the giving of religious books and laying hands. HHJ Eady held that:

> If the case is one of direct discrimination, then the focus on the reason why the less favourable treatment occurred should permit an Employment Tribunal to identify those case where the treatment is not because of the manifestation of the religion or belief but because of the inappropriate manner of the manifestation.[39]

The employee usually tells the Tribunal they were dismissed (or suffered another detriment) because of their opinions. The employer typically responds that they were not dismissed for a belief but for its manifestation – the unpleasant and unwelcome way in which the employee spoke about others.

The distinction between these analyses is that it is unlawful to sanction or dismiss a person because of their opinions (especially where those opinions are expressed moderately). It is, however, entirely lawful to sanction or dismiss a member of staff because their behaviour crosses the line into the active harassment of other staff or customers. This is, once again, "the reason why" question.[40]

The Tribunal's task is to understand why a sanction took place, whether it was for the reason of the employee's opinion (which will usually be unlawful) or for the reason of the employee's conduct (which may well be lawful). In a typical conflicts of rights case, the Court will focus carefully on the reasons for the employer's decision to sanction or dismiss. They have to consider whether it was because of someone's opinions or because of something they said or did. Judges will listen to both sides and consider which explanation best fits what actually happened.

Proselytising

A number of the cases where the distinction between opinion and manifestation/conduct have been at the clearest have involved Christian employees either refusing to carry out services intended for non-Christian customers or

38 *Page v NHS Trust Development Authority* [2021] EWCA Civ 255, para 68.
39 *Wasteney v East London NHS Foundation Trust* [2016] ICR 643, para 55.
40 *Essop v Home Office* [2015] EWCA Civ 609, para 57. And Chapter 2.

proselytising among their fellow employees. In *Ladele v London Borough of Islington*,[41] the Court of Appeal considered the case of a Christian marriage registrar who argued that a requirement to conduct a same-sex civil ceremony was in breach of her right to freedom of religion under Article 9 of the European Convention on Human Rights. She believed that same-sex unions were contrary to God's will and that it would be wrong for her to participate in the creation of an institution equivalent to marriage between a same-sex couple. Because of her refusal to agree to be designated as a registrar of civil partnerships, disciplinary proceedings were brought, culminating in the loss of her job. Dismissal, she argued, was discrimination under the then protection against discrimination on grounds of belief.[42] She won at first instance in the Employment Tribunal. However, the employer successfully appealed to the Employment Appeal Tribunal, and the EAT's reasoning was upheld by both the Court of Appeal and, ultimately, the European Court of Human Rights.[43]

In the Court of Appeal, Neuberger LJ considered Ms Ladele's claim of direct discrimination which was based on a witness for the employer who had argued that Islington could not employ a registrar who does not wish to participate in civil partnership duties. Lord Justice Neuberger held that

> This statement was directed not to Ms Ladele's belief with regard to civil partnerships, but to the manifestation of that belief, namely her refusal to conduct such partnership duties.[44]

Ms Ladele argued that it would have been open to her employer to keep her at work while simply freeing her from any obligation to carry out same-sex services. The Court of Appeal held, and the ECtHR accepted, that such a private opt-out would have damaged the public authority's attempts to be an organisation "wholly committed to the promotion of equal opportunities and to requiring all its employees to act in a way which does not discriminate against others". In other words, Ms Ladele's religious freedom could not be protected without diminishing the rights of others to have their relationships recognised.

In a second case heard at the same time by the ECtHR, the Human Rights Court considered the case of a Coptic Christian employee of British Airways, Ms Eweida, who claimed that BA's dress code requiring jewellery to be concealed discriminated against her as a Christian since it did not allow her

41 *Ladele v London Borough of Islington* [2009] EWCA Civ 1357.

42 Employment Equality (Religion or Belief) Regulations 2003, now incorporated into Equality Act 2010.

43 *Eweida and Ors v United Kingdom* [2013] ECHR 37.

44 *Ladele v Islington*, para 35.

to wear a cross prominently. Eweida had been unsuccessful in proceedings before the Court of Appeal, with Sedley LJ holding that any indirect discrimination against her had been proportionate and justified. For seven years, Ms Eweida had worked for the company without complaining. Ms Eweida had a preference for wearing a cross, but nothing in her religion required it. She had the choice of working without displaying her cross or of maintaining her job without loss of pay in a private role. Further, her treatment had not been indirectly discriminatory since the organisation was a huge employer and only one employee had been affected. While the purpose of indirect discrimination law was to prevent seemingly neutral requirements from being used in ways which achieved discriminatory impacts, the way in which equality laws on both sides of the Atlantic had for many years sought to do this is by seeing, first, whether a group was adversely affected. Mrs Eweida was all alone in suffering a detriment, and for that reason, her claim failed.[45]

On the long-running issue of the relationship between the manifestations of belief and believers themselves, and the protection afforded to each, the ECtHR had this to say:

> Even where the belief in question attains the required level of cogency and importance, it cannot be said that every act which is in some way inspired, motivated or influenced by it constitutes a "manifestation" of the belief. Thus, for example, acts or omissions which do not directly express the belief concerned or which are only remotely connected to a precept of faith fall outside the protection of art.9(1). In order to count as a "manifestation" within the meaning of art.9, the act in question must be intimately linked to the religion or belief. An example would be an act of worship or devotion which forms part of the practice of a religion or belief in a generally recognised form. However, the manifestation of religion or belief is not limited to such acts; the existence of a sufficiently close and direct nexus between the act and the underlying belief must be determined on the facts of each case. In particular, there is no requirement on the applicant to establish that he or she acted in fulfilment of a duty mandated by the religion in question.[46]

The Human Rights Court disagreed with the Court of Appeal and found that Ms Eweida's treatment had been indirectly discriminatory and disproportionate. Her desire to manifest her belief was a fundamental right; a healthy democratic society needs to tolerate and sustain pluralism and diversity; and it was

45 *Eweida v British Airways Plc* [2010] EWCA Civ 80, paras 19, 37.
46 *Eweida v United Kingdom* [2013] IRLR 231, para 82.

of particular value to an individual who has made religion a central tenet of her life to be able to communicate that belief to others.

In *Ladele*, the courts were considering competing rights in what was effectively a zero-sum game: the advancement of Ms Ladele's rights could only come at the expense of other people's rights. Accordingly, dismissal was proportionate. By contrast, in *Eweida,* there was "no evidence of any real encroachment on the interests of others",[47] and the applicant's right to manifest her religious beliefs should have been protected.

47 *Eweida v United Kingdom*, para 94.

7 Instructions to keep silent

This chapter addresses what happens when a person remains in employment; however, the employer seeks to restrict the employee's freedom of expression, for example, by prohibiting them from organising an event around a particular theme or by preventing them from discussing a certain topic with other employees or the press, etc. Certain consequences might follow; for example, the employee might complain to the Court and seek an injunction upholding their freedom of expression. Or, the employee might continue to speak, and the employer dismisses them. Was the dismissal unfair?

Much of the public commentary around employee-silencing concerns educational bodies; however, in reality, the practice occurs much more widely. So that, for example:

- In the 1970s, it was common for trade union organisations to seek to prohibit political propaganda put out by far-right groups, even at election time, for example, by instructing their members to prevent far-right political broadcasts from being aired by the stations for which the members worked;[1]
- Previous chapters have cited the example from the 2000s of trade unions calling for the dismissal of a member of far-right parties where that member worked for a private sector bus company;[2]
- In more recent times, there have been complaints of people being denied speaking platforms in non-educational settings, for example, allegations of gender-critical political activists being prevented from addressing conferences put on by trade bodies of which they were members;[3]
- On the other side of the same issue, there have been press reports of employers instructing trans students,[4] or members of workplace LGBT

1 D. Renton, *Never Again: Rock Against Racism and the Anti-Nazi League 1976–1982* (London: Routledge, 2018), p 95.
2 *Redfearn v the United Kingdom* [2012] ECHR 1878.
3 *Clare v Craft Potters Association*, ET case no 2204566/2022.
4 'University of Bristol Not "Uncomfortable" Disciplining Trans Activist,' *BBC News*, 11 February 2022.

DOI: 10.4324/9781032724263-7

groups,[5] to keep silent and desist from criticising gender-critical employees and to threaten those who express their opinions with disciplinary sanction;[6] and

- In 2022, the Glasgow Sheriff Court heard a case brought by the Billy Graham Evangelistic Association after their booking of the largest exhibition centre in Scotland was cancelled. Glasgow City Council gave as its reason for the cancellation the homophobic and Islamophobic comments previously made by one of the event's main speakers. On the facts, this was found to be direct discrimination on grounds of the complainant's religious beliefs of evangelical Protestantism, and unlawful, and a total of £97,000 was ordered in damages.[7]

In the case of *Nenkova-Lalova v Bulgaria*, the ECtHR had to choose between two contending reasons for a journalist's dismissal. The journalist complained that she had been sanctioned for exposing corrupt practices by the government during a radio show. The Bulgarian government insisted that she had been legitimately dismissed for ignoring a management instruction not to interview a fellow journalist, Ms V N. The instructions related solely to who Ms Nenkova-Lalova should interview and not the subject of the discussion, nor had there been any attempt to censor what she discussed. The ECtHR concluded that there had been a breach of article 10, but it had been justified.[8]

In *Kudeshkina v Russia*, a judge of 18 years standing was permitted to suspend her role as a judge and campaign for a seat in the Russian State Duma. She described the Russian courts as subject to commercial, political, and personal manipulation. The Judiciary Qualification Board terminated her appointment. The ECtHR notes that the statements the judge had made were not devoid of factual grounds, rather, they were fair comments on a matter of great public importance. Her fears as regards the impartiality of the Moscow City Court were justified. It concluded that her removal from judicial office had been an unjustified infringement of her rights pursuant to article 10.[9]

Silencing: criminal behaviour

If an employer in England or Wales was asked to accept their employee participating in events where the employee or their supporters had a violent record, the employer's obligation to uphold freedom of expression would not

5 L. Brooks, 'Edinburgh LGBT+ Committee Resigns in Row Over Speakers at Feminist Meeting,' *The Guardian*, 6 June 2019.

6 N. Badshah, 'University Defends "Academic Freedoms" After Calls to Sack Professor,' *The Guardian*, 7 October 2021.

7 *Billy Graham Evangelistic Association v Scottish Event Campus Limited* [2022] Sh Ct GLW 33.

8 *Nenkova-Lalova v Bulgaria* [2012] ECHR 2058, para 60.

9 *Kudeshkina v Russia* (2011) 52 EHRR37, paras 84, 95–7.

extend to requiring an employer to keep an employee in employment where they were organising events at which criminal behaviour was likely, and with which the employer would be associated.

However, it is worth bearing in mind that the majority of what its opponents characterise as offensive language does not breach criminal law. For example, in February 2020, the High Court heard a complaint concerning Harry Miller. He had accused trans rights supporters of "building an army", told people who disagreed with them that their views were "crap", and posted messages belittling trans people. After two dozen such tweets and a complaint, Mr Miller was visited by a police officer, who recorded the events as hate incidents. The High Court held that the tweets had not contravened the criminal law and that the police were wrong to have recorded Miller's tweets as a hate crime. Free speech, the Court insisted, protects even speech which is "opaque, profane, or unsophisticated".[10] The decision was reversed on appeal (i.e., the Court held that the officer had been acting correctly in recording Mr Miller's conduct as hate speech), but the Court of Appeal nevertheless endorsed the High Court's findings that Miller's tweets had not been criminal.[11] Such expression might well be pejorative,[12] but it was not criminal.

Moreover, on occasion, even behaviour which is criminal or tortious will not necessarily make an infringement of article 10 proportionate. So, in *Grigoriades v Greece*, a Greek soldier had been punished after which he wrote a letter criticising the army as basing its authority on a hierarchy of fear.[13]

Under Greek military law, insulting the army was criminal conduct, and the soldier was sentenced to three months' imprisonment. On application to Strasbourg, the European Court of Human Rights found that the soldier's treatment had been disproportionate for several reasons, including that the criticisms of the army had not been circulated widely but had only been disclosed to the soldier's senior officer.

Silencing following management instruction: article 10

In the 2019 case of *Kuteh v Dartford and Gravesend NHS Trust*, the Court of Appeal considered the case of a nurse who was expected to carry out up to 12 assessments per day of patients who were due to undergo surgery. Patients complained that she had been discussing religion with them. The Claimant's Matron, Ms Gill, instructed Ms Kuteh to stop discussing her religious views

10 *Miller, R (on the application of) v The College of Policing and Anor* [2020] EWHC 225, para 250.

11 *Miller, R (on the application of) v The College of Policing and Anor* [2021] EWCA Civ 1926, para 70.

12 See, for example, Keira McCormack's successful complaint to the UK Press Complaints Commission about an article which appeared in the Northern Ireland newspaper, *Sunday Life*, which used various belittling terms, including calling her a "tranny". Adjudication issued 4 January 2020.

13 *Grigoriades v Greece* [1997] ECHR 93.

with her patients. However, she continued, causing one patient to describe her language as "very bizarre" and "like a Monty Python skit".[14] Ms Kuteh was dismissed for failing to follow management instructions. Her claims for unfair dismissal were dismissed, and her appeals failed.

Silencing following instruction: can the distinction between manifestation and belief survive?

Most employees accused of ignoring instructions not to proselytise have challenged their dismissal not through article 10 but through the Equality Act and its protection of religion or belief. In *Chondol v Liverpool City Council*,[15] the EAT heard an appeal brought by a social worker who was found to have been fairly dismissed by a local authority after he promoted his religious beliefs at work. On one occasion, he gave a Bible to a service user. On another occasion, he engaged with another services user who complained to the council that Mr Chondol was "talking about God and church and crap like that".[16] The EAT accepted the findings of the original Tribunal that Mr Chondol had been dismissed not for his opinions but on account of his behaviour: "He showed no appreciation of the important boundaries between his position as a friend and his role as a social worker".[17]

In *Trayhorn v The Secretary of State for Justice*, the Employment Appeal Tribunal considered the case of a Pentecostal Christian who had been instructed by his employer not to preach at chapel services after complaints from an LGBT co-ordinator. Three months later, in defiance of the ban, in a service in a prison holding a large number of sex offenders, he quoted a passage from the Bible condemning certain sexual behaviour and speaking of repentance. A prisoner complained.

Mr Trayhorn was given a warning for his conduct and complained to the Employment Tribunal that he had suffered a detriment on account of religion or belief. The Tribunal found that the issue was the insensitive manifestation of the Claimant's belief. The relevant PCP required all employees to adhere to the relevant policies which were set out in the prison's Equality of Treatment Policy. If this had amounted to indirect discrimination, the discrimination was, in any event, proportionate within the prison in light of the need to maintain order there. The EAT agreed, accepting the finding that the prison's policy did not disadvantage Christians singly or as a group.[18]

A slightly different outcome was reached in *Higgs v Farmor's School,* where a school administrator had posted on Facebook claims that by promoting sex

14 *Kuteh v Dartford and Gravesend NHS Trust* [2019] EWCA Civ 818, para 68.
15 *Chondol v Liverpool City Council* [2009] EAT 0298/08.
16 *Chondol v Liverpool*, para 9.
17 *Chondol v Liverpool*, para 31.
18 *Trayhorn v The Secretary of State for Justice* [2017] EAT 0304/16, para 80.

education, the government was "brainwashing our children" and obliging them to accept LGBT and trans rights. The Tribunal rejected her claim of unfair dismissal, finding that there was no causal connection between the Claimant's belief and her punishment. She was dismissed for having used florid and provocative language and for the Respondent's conclusion that, even if her views were not extreme, so radical was her action that people associated with the school would have assumed that she held different, extreme, and unacceptable opinions. At the EAT, that decision was overturned and remitted for consideration, but the Claimant's victory was partial – the case was remitted to the same Tribunal. The essential legal flaw, as analysed by the EAT, was that the Tribunal had refused to acknowledge the close nexus between the Claimant's Facebook posts and her protected beliefs. They had been required to consider, but failed to address, whether the Respondent's actions were related to the manifestation of the Claimant's protected beliefs or were due to a justified objection to the manner of that manifestation. The EAT set out various matters of guidance which are of general significance:

(1) First, the foundational nature of the rights must be recognised: the freedom to manifest belief (religious or otherwise) and to express views relating to that belief are essential rights in any democracy, whether or not the belief in question is popular or mainstream and even if its expression may offend.
(2) Second, those rights are, however, qualified. The manifestation of belief, and free expression, will be protected but not where the law permits the limitation or restriction of such manifestation or expression to the extent necessary for the protection of the rights and freedoms of others. Where such limitation or restriction is objectively justified given the manner of the manifestation or expression, that is not, properly understood, action taken because of, or relating to, the exercise of the rights in question but is by reason of the objectionable manner of the manifestation or expression.
(3) Whether a limitation or restriction is objectively justified will always be context-specific. The fact that the issue arises within a relationship of employment will be relevant, but different considerations will inevitably arise, depending on the nature of that employment.
(4) It will always be necessary to ask (per *Bank Mellat*):[19] (i) whether the objective the employer seeks to achieve is sufficiently important to justify the limitation of the right in question; (ii) whether the limitation is rationally connected to that objective; (iii) whether a less intrusive limitation might be imposed without undermining the achievement of the objective in question; and (iv) whether, balancing the severity of the

19 *Bank Mellatt v HM Treasury (No 2)* [2014] AC 700, para 68–76.

limitation on the rights of the worker concerned against the importance of the objective, the former outweighs the latter.

(5) In answering those questions, within the context of a relationship of employment, the considerations identified by the intervenor are likely to be relevant, such that regard should be had to: (i) the content of the manifestation; (ii) the tone used; (iii) the extent of the manifestation; (iv) the worker's understanding of the likely audience; (v) the extent and nature of the intrusion on the rights of others, and any consequential impact on the employer's ability to run its business; (vi) whether the worker has made clear that the views expressed are personal, or whether they might be seen as representing the views of the employer, and whether that might present a reputational risk; (vii) whether there is a potential power imbalance given the nature of the worker's position or role and that of those whose rights are intruded upon; (viii) the nature of the employer's business, in particular where there is a potential impact on vulnerable service users or clients; (ix) whether the limitation imposed is the least intrusive measure open to the employer.[20]

The judgment in *Higgs* is of particular significance since the judge was the Honourable Mrs Justice Eady, President of the EAT, and, therefore, the most senior specialist discrimination lawyer in Britain.

Although the decision in *Higgs* concerned a transphobic administrator, and the rights and wrongs of the decision have generally been debated through the lens of that issue, the judgment is of much wider significance. Potentially, its impact may well be to collapse the distinction between beliefs which are protected and their manifestation, which is not. Once we accept that there may be a close nexus between a person's beliefs and their manifestation, and we understand that (where that nexus is identified) the manifestation too is protected from discrimination, then all sorts of discriminatory rules which the employment courts have long upheld, are going to be much harder to defend. A ban on Muslim headscarves, for example, may well come to be recognised for what it is: a piece of discrimination against Muslim women which – being direct discrimination against them for behaviour closely connected to their beliefs – cannot be justified and is unlawful.

At the time that this manuscript is being drafted, the immediate future appears to be one in which opinions and beliefs are going to be receiving much more active protection from the Employment Tribunal than they had been a mere decade ago.[21]

20 *Higgs v Farmor's School* [2023] EAT 89, para 94.

21 One of the first high-profile post-*Higgs* decisions was *Miller v University of Bristol* [2024] case no 1400780/2022, in which anti-Zionist opinions were found to be protected.

Index

For Product Safety Concerns and Information please contact our EU representative GPSR@taylorandfrancis.com
Taylor & Francis Verlag GmbH, Kaufingerstraße 24, 80331 München, Germany

www.ingramcontent.com/pod-product-compliance
Lightning Source LLC
LaVergne TN
LVHW010938110826
845149LV00013B/2656

* 9 7 8 1 0 3 2 7 2 4 2 9 4 *